CREATIVE SELF-HEALTH

A Consciousness-Based Approach

DR. LORI-ANN GERTONSON
AND
TONI MANDARA

The Gertonson Institute

ISBN: 978-1-7332956-1-1
Albany, CA 94706

Cover design by:
SelfPubBookCovers.com/AnaCruzArts

Inside image design: Lynn Bradshaw

To the Spirit of Creative Self-Health that flows through all there is and will be

.

CONTENTS

ACKNOWLEDGMENTS

When we began to talk about this project we had no idea of the many people who would show up to nourish its creation. It is a great pleasure to acknowledge those who generously shared their time and talent. Toni's wonderful friend and author, Lyndra Hearn Antonson, was unfailingly supportive in her feedback as the first draft reader. Finding Leigh Saffold of Blue Pen Agency to help us learn to navigate the publishing world was a boon! Her professionalism is outstanding. We also want to thank Laura Miller for her editing expertise.

Our illustrators, Seneca Beth Miller and Lynn Bradshaw, gave us the all important core rendering of how Spiritual Intelligence is both source and resource for the human experience. So many friends were a part of the cheerleading squad in the development of the book, but none more so than our colleague and dear friend, Marcel Allbritton.

We would also like to thank our book cover artist, Ana Cruz.

From Toni:

Finally, this book could not exist without the expertise, love, and patience of my co-author, Dr. Lori-Ann Gertonson. She is a close friend, trusted advisor, and healer par excellence. We have traveled a long and unexpected road together, and it is my honor to have done my best to tell the tale.

From Lori:

My heartfelt appreciation goes to my co-author and dear friend Toni Mandara. She is the embodiment of humility and grace. I cannot thank her enough for her dedication to this project and her exceptional writing skills. She took our ideas and concepts and so eloquently turned them into words on a page. I am honored to have travelled together on this journey. I also want to thank my family for their continued love and support.

INTRODUCTION

*"The doctor of the future will give no medicine, but
will interest his or her patients in the care of the
human frame, in a proper diet, and the cause and
prevention of disease."*

-*Thomas Edison*

Dear Reader,

If you are reading this book, chances are you
already know a lot about what it takes to be healthy.
You understand the importance of a good diet and
regular exercise. You can even recite a laundry list of
what to do and what not to do when it comes to good
health, i.e., smoking is a no-no, while it's good to get
enough sleep every night.

You've learned enough about the unique responses
of your own body to know not to drink that
caffeinated drink after 4pm, or to remember to tell
your doctor the names of medications you've taken in
the past with poor results. You try to keep up with
the latest news from medical science about what
works and what doesn't when it comes to health, but

the contradictions and trends can get pretty confusing.

At the same time, you may have struggled with common issues like weight, depression, or coping with the stresses of everyday life. Like so many of us, you or someone you know has experienced a major illness or chronic condition that traditional medicine seems unable to effectively address or explain.

This book is about what's been missing in your search for better health and healing. In a time of skyrocketing health care costs and the rise of chronic conditions, we will show you why reforming our present health care system will not bring you the healing you desire.

This book is about shifting your orientation from health care consumer to Self-Health Creator. Creative Self-Health is the process of taking action on your own behalf to return to a natural state of dynamic, vibrant healthy wholeness.

Your innate tendency is always in the direction of wholeness, but for most of us, this tendency has become blocked or obstructed. We'll be talking about how to identify and release the blocks to wholeness, and how deepening your experiences of self-care will put you in touch with the power of an inner healing system that operates without drugs, surgeries, or side effects.

And most of all, this book is about you, the "Self" in Creative Self-Health. Because once you understand who *you* are, you will also understand that you were born to create the beautiful, empowered and happy life you have only imagined up to now. You will become aware of yourself as more than just a physical body. You will begin to see that health is not about finding the miracle cure or the miracle drug, but that *you* are the miracle. It is about recognizing that when you have developed the proper mindset in the right environment, and supplied yourself with the right resources, you can heal yourself.

The term Creative Self-Health links this new understanding of you to a different orientation towards health. It shifts the focus on health from a doctor-centered strategy to the power of healing from within. It is about finding and eliminating the cause of disease and illness, not just quieting the symptoms. The "Creative" part of Creative Self-Health is resourced from what we call Spiritual Intelligence, that consciousness that creates and animates all there is. For some, Spiritual Intelligence may be equated with God or Divine Spirit. For others, it could be expressed as Universal Love or simply nature. It is Spiritual Intelligence that gives us our innate capability for healing.

This idea of healing from within is rooted in ancient wisdom, and now verified by the science of quantum physics. In order to develop your new understanding of Creative Self-Health, we will explore both the ancient traditions of healing and the miraculous discoveries of quantum science.

While some of these ideas may seem strange at first, please be patient as you read through and consider the possibility that there is far more to you than you may have known. We will also explore the "Health" in Creative Self-Health, and why health is much more than our mainstream cultural beliefs about it.

Finally, while this book describes certain practices that support healing, it is important to understand that healing itself is a lifetime commitment. We are talking about processes that are non-linear, with many overlapping stages. Our practices are only tools, for Creative Self-Health is experiential and unique to each individual.

Should you decide to take charge of your own

health and follow these practices, you will experience healing from the inside out. You will connect with a greater part of yourself and learn to trust it as it leads you toward wholeness. All that is required is your open mind and willingness to start the process.

If you're ready, let's begin...

Dr. Lori-Ann Gertonson
Toni Mandara

CHAPTER ONE

The Truth About Health and Healing

*"The cure of the part should not be attempted
without the cure of the whole. No attempt should be
made to cure the body without the soul...For this is
the great error of our day in the treatment of the
human body, that physicians first separate the soul
from the body."*

-Plato

You have the ability to heal yourself. If you doubt
this, consider what happens when you cut your
finger. The wound seals and leaves no trace. You
seldom think about that cut once the skin has closed
over the area and the pain is gone. At the internal
cellular level, there is an automatic process going on
that involves regenerating the tissues. As long as

there is no block or obstruction that interferes with the process, you do not have to do anything in order for healing to happen. You were designed this way, with everything that is needed for healing as part of the structure of your being. Let's call this design your inner healer.

On a larger scale, what happens when a crisis such as a broken leg occurs? This is the kind of circumstance that our conventional Western medical system works very well with, resetting the bone and stabilizing the leg with a cast so that the body is aligned to begin healing itself. Once alignment is accomplished, the healing begins.

Of course, the process was served by the expertise of the physician, and the support of others who provided emotional, mental, and practical help. Together, this team worked to provide the alignment needed for the inner healer to do its work. The doctor set the bone, but the intelligence within the body did the healing.

Unfortunately, our modern orientation to health places far more emphasis on the need to rely on external fixes given by a doctor than the natural ability of our human system to heal. Shifting our orientation to a Creative Self-Health model is about choosing alignment with the inner healer as a lifestyle, rather than just a response to a health crisis. Why does this matter?

While there is no doubt it can save lives in acute situations, conventional Western medicine is limited in what it can do to stem the tide of distress and chronic disease, particularly the kinds of lifestyle diseases that have become epidemic in our country today. In fact, conventional Western medicine is itself the cause of an inordinate number of deaths and illnesses annually.

The overwhelming evidence for this can be seen in the following statistics from a study by primary healthcare advocate Barbara Starfield, MD, MPH, published in 2000 in the Journal of the American Medical Association:

- 106,000 deaths every year from adverse drug reactions (taken as prescribed)
- 80,000 from infections acquired in hospitals
- 45,000 due to other medical errors
- 12,000 due to unnecessary surgeries
- 7,000 due to medication errors in hospitals

That means 225, 000 deaths per year are induced inadvertently by a physician, surgeon, or medical treatment or diagnostic procedure. The term for this type of death is iatrogenic. Iatrogenic deaths add up to make our own medical care system the third largest killer of Americans, just after heart disease and cancer.

There seems to be no cure for lifestyle-based conditions such as obesity, diabetes, heart disease, and some cancers. It has been said that ours is a sickness care system rather than a health care system, and despite political debates around reform, we are getting sicker. How can this be? According to wellness lifestyle doctor James Chestnut, D.C., the medical establishment is just like the fire department. When your house is burning down, all they care about is putting out the fire. They use axes and high-pressure water hoses to do this, leaving your home in shambles after the fire is out. But when you want to rebuild or maintain your home, you don't call the fire department. You call the experts who understand how to keep your home in good working condition and prevent emergencies like fires.

We have talked about the body's ability to heal itself. Simply put, healing comes from within. We'll be going into more detail about what this means, but right now it's enough to note that our bodies are brilliantly designed to maintain and restore healthy balance. Instead of maximizing our innate healing abilities, conventional Western medicine focuses on finding cures by manipulating the body through drugs or surgeries. From this perspective, a cure means we must alter the natural processes of the human system by artificial means. The cure orientation leads to a rise in surgical or drug solutions to take the place of natural human processes. C-sections and hysterectomies become far more common than necessary, while natural childbirth is unusual. The poisoning of the body through radiation and chemotherapy becomes a routine and accepted way to prolong life, while the impact of the destruction of healthy cells and the risk of death from these treatments is just collateral damage. This approach to health and healing leaves conventional Western medicine only partially effective. It stands pretty much in direct opposition to the more vital orientation of healing espoused in ancient healing traditions for thousands of years, a view that approaches the human system as a living dynamic organism that is more than the sum of its parts.

The following chart compares these two points of view:

Healing vs. Cure

Healing	Cure
Vitalistic	Mechanistic
Internal	External
Natural	Artificial
Cause oriented	Symptom based
Wholistic	Reductionistic
Integrating	Disintegrating
Inside – out	Outside – in
Expressive	Suppressive
Creative	Destructive
Life is consciousness	Life is chemistry
In-line with Divine	Kill the messenger
Quantum Physics	Newtonian Physics
Well-being is natural state-remove interferences	Alters natural state
Allowing	Forcing
Growth	Death
Connection	Separation
Whole is greater than sum of the parts	Whole is sum of the individual parts
Inner power oriented	Victim oriented
Well-being	Disease
Awakening	Deadening
Active	Passive
	We "cure" pickles, leather, etc.

We believe that conventional Western medicine is limited by its outdated mechanistic approach to the science of health and healing. Even in acute situations where conventional care is most effective, its limited understanding of healing can lead to life-altering disability.

Consider the true story of Mitchell May, a young man who was involved in a catastrophic car accident at age twenty-one. He was pronounced dead at the scene of the accident with broken bones in forty places and punctured lungs. May was resuscitated, yet weeks later his situation was dire. He was suffering from systemic infection and an army of seventy orthopedic doctors insisted they must amputate his leg if he wanted to live. May refused, and with the help of a gifted healer, he learned to regenerate bone, muscle, and nerves from the inside out. Called a medical miracle by his doctors, May's recovery was the result of choosing healing rather than the "cure" of an amputating his leg. Today, Mitchell May teaches others about healing into wholeness based on his experiences. May's work aligns with the radically new information about healing that comes from the science of quantum physics. This information confirms the wisdom of ancient traditions, and goes beyond to offer a scientifically based vision not only of who we really are, but what we are capable of in terms of healing.

You are More Than a Physical Body

The science that supports and confirms what ancient wisdom has told us for millennia is called quantum physics. Quantum physics shows us a new way to understand the nature of the universe and how it works at the most fundamental level. Before the discoveries of quantum physics, our medical system and much of our understanding of the basic nature of reality was shaped by the theories of seventeenth century scientists such as Rene Descartes and Sir Isaac Newton. Newtonian physics told us the mechanistic view was reality. There was matter and there was energy, each existing separately and according to certain physical laws. We experience the body as being present on a material level. This level is what our five senses tell us is reality. From the Newtonian point of view, everything we experience-thoughts, feelings, intuition, etc.-are generated within the material realm of the body. From this viewpoint, you *are* your physical body.

Then another famous scientist, Albert Einstein, introduced a radical challenge to this theory. Researcher and author Dr. Joe Dispenza explains that contrary to the theories of Newton and Descartes, Einstein's work showed there was virtually no fundamental difference between energy and matter. This finding changed our previous understanding of how the universe operates.

Simply put, if matter (i.e. physical body) and energy (emotions, thought, spirit, consciousness) are one and the same, you are more than what you experience on a material, physical level. Quantum physicists went on to discover that at the atomic level, we are 99.99999 percent energy and .00001 percent matter (physical). At this vast quantum energetic level, all possibilities exist.

Many ancient wisdom traditions express this understanding of humans as energetic (spiritual) beings. Further, these traditions recognize our true nature as an expression of a single, shared Spiritual Intelligence. In quantum science terms, we are part of a quantum field of consciousness. "You, like all of us, broadcast a distinct energy pattern or signature." Dr. Dispenza explains. "In fact, everything material is always emitting specific patterns of energy. And this energy carries information. Your fluctuating states of mind consciously or unconsciously change that signature on a moment-to-moment basis because you are more than a physical body; you are a consciousness using a body to express different levels of mind."

In the twenty-first century we have finally reached a point where science and mysticism are beginning to agree that there is an energetic Intelligence that influences and shapes the material existence of the cosmos in any and all directions. The implications are truly mind-bending.

Remember the old Star Trek series where we were introduced to the concept of a holodeck? The holodeck existed on board the starship Enterprise. It provided a multi-dimensional, multi-sensory simulation of any environment the crew wanted to experience. Want to go to a South Pacific island? Just program the energetic patterns into the holodeck and step into your fantasy. The world of the holodeck was as material as our everyday reality, yet created from energetic patterns stored in the ship's computer. What physicists are now finding is that science fiction was not so fictional after all.

At the quantum level, you exist as a holographic projection from Spiritual Intelligence of several energetic fields that include the physical, emotional, mental, archetypal and spiritual parts of you. Each of us is simultaneously projected by that Intelligence and existing within it. In other words, the material world as we know it can be considered our own holodeck, programmed by Spiritual Intelligence. Our physical bodies are multi-dimensional, multi-sensory energetic patterns within that Intelligence.

While the physical body encompasses the density of the material, the other energy fields are experienced as vibration, thought, feeling, intuition, knowing and subtle influences, i.e. chi or prana.

Far more than just a physical body, from a Self-Health perspective, you look like this:

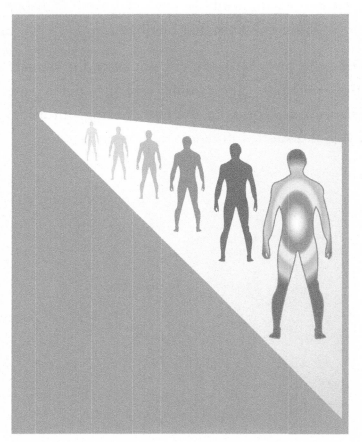

Within the projection of Spiritual Intelligence, the different individual bodies depicted above represent the different energy fields contained within the physical body (figure on the far right). As the illustration indicates, all the energetic fields (spiritual, archetypal, mental, emotional, subtle energies) are accessed from within the physical body. Each field has a specific purpose that supports health and wholeness.

As described by author Jean Houston, archetypal energies provide guidance for living fully. This field is part of the human collective, meaning it belongs to all of us, like an easily recognized model of certain roles we play in society. For instance, we all have an instinctive sense of the archetypal mother role and its importance to us as human beings.

The mental field is where thoughts determine meaning, influence activities and create actions. We will interpret choices about health and healing depending on the meaning assigned to those choices by the mental field.

When you feel strong emotions, the emotional field is generating an experience that can profoundly impact the entire human system within. The emotional field often determines the quality of our everyday life.

Finally, there is the subtle energetic field, in some traditions called chi or prana. This field directs and channels the flow of vitality in the physical body.

These invisible energetic forces profoundly impact our lives, yet we tend to focus on physical reality as if it was the only reality. It is easy to understand why this happens. Think of how projection happens at a movie theater absorbs us in what is happening onscreen. We focus our attention on the screen and experience the story and actions of the characters as if they are reality. We forget about the script, the projector and the many other elements that went into making the movie look, sound, and feel real. And of course, without the writers, cinematographers, sound and production crew and many others, the movie would not exist. In the same way, the energetic aspects of being all create the physical aspect. This explains why emotional trauma and mental stress are known to be sources of physical illness. In fact, the energetic vibrations of the mental, emotional, archetypal and spiritual fields are just as real and influential to health as the physical.

Louise Hay in her book *You Can Heal Your Body*ₗ describes how different mental patterns can create dis-ease and relates these patterns to specific body areas and/or illnesses. For example, lower back problems often have a mental pattern around money, or relationships. There is usually a feeling of a lack of support in one of these areas. Neck problems may have a pattern of thought that represents stubbornness or inflexibility. You can address these issues from a Self-Health perspective and access the power of the inner healer by first understanding the true source, or mental pattern of the physical symptoms on an energetic level. Next you correct the thought pattern to be in alignment with the flow of Spiritual Intelligence. Finally, trust that the healing is already taking place. This is a process to be repeated until healing is complete. It can occur in a quantum moment, or it may take time and repetition.

Because you are a being who is infused with the energetic flow of the infinite, the wisdom of the ages can be accessed from within. Spiritual Intelligence is the true source of your being, and the source of all healing. Given this model of what you are made of, you may have already guessed that healing is a multi-layered process that can happen at different levels across energetic fields. The good news is that a moment of high level healing in the greater part of you can bring wholeness to the entire human system. This type of quantum moment (or leap) occurs unpredictably, yet always affects deep change. Toni shares one such moment from her life:

> Many years ago, I was attending a workshop. I had come alone, and knew none

of the other participants at the beginning of the program. Over the weekend, I began to learn about the other participants and appreciate what they shared of their life experiences. One who had particularly impressed me was a young man who introduced himself as a pediatrician. With a bit of embarrassment, he confided that babies just somehow magically became calm when he held them.

On the last day of the program, we gathered for a group exercise that involved moving around the room from partner to partner, each partner putting a hand over the other partner's heart and silently sending loving energy. I moved around the room partnering with various people, enjoying the sweetness of the exercise, until at one point I found myself partnered with the young pediatrician.

As with all the other partners, he put his hand over my heart. Then something extraordinary happened. I can only describe it as an immense channel opening into my heart, bringing with it a flood of Love. I capitalize the word, because the quality of this Love was not human. It was not a feeling so much as an experience. It was unconditional, pure, neither romantic nor parental. It was impersonal yet intensely personalized.

It was as if I were receiving a transmission from Spiritual Intelligence itself. There was movement, flow, vibration, light, and beauty. As the immensity and infinite nature of this Love continued to pour into my heart, I went into shock, unable to stay open to it for more than a few moments. I felt myself close and the experience once again became just another nice workshop exercise. At the end of the exercise, no one else seemed to report anything unusual, but I was so moved that I pulled the doctor to the side and told him I now understood what those babies were feeling when he held them. He was clearly not just a doctor, but a true healer.

Though I'd spent some years meditating and doing other spiritual practices, this experience of Love was earthshaking to me. I now know it as a gift of grace, a quantum moment. Never again could I discard the understanding that there was more to life than this material realm. The something more was a lived experience. I had stood, for one quantum moment, in the vibration of a Love beyond words. And life would never be the same.

Quantum moments are available to all of us. They

seem to occur most frequently within a context of alignment and openness to the vast potentials of the inner energetic fields. To experience this self that is more than a physical body, you must be willing to shift your orientation from seeking external cures to accessing the power of the inner healer.

Healing is a Choice

When we understand ourselves as more than a physical body, we start to tap into the power of the inner healer. We see that our choices can guide us to healing, and not just the choices about what we eat or how often we exercise. Our thoughts and feelings create biochemical responses in our bodies. Our habitual thought patterns, or belief systems, are constantly impacting the physical body and our experiences of life. On the face of it, life often presents us with situations and circumstances that we don't like or desire. We can, however, choose how we respond to life. This is what it means to take responsibility. " Responsibility is not burden, fault, praise, blame, credit, shame, or guilt," self-development expert Werner Erhard writes. "Responsibility starts with the willingness to deal with the situation from and with the point of view, whether at the moment realized or not, that you are the source of what you are, what you do, and what you have. "

We can take responsibility by understanding that our lifestyle choices, including our thoughts, emotions, and attitudes, create the biological and environmental signals that control stress levels and so much more. We can choose to align with Spiritual Intelligence in order to activate our inner healer. On Star Trek, the crew accessed the ship's computer in order to program a holodeck experience. We can choose to change our experience by accessing Spiritual Intelligence from within to reset the program we are living.

Healing Comes From Within

Imagine an ancient door, its warm wooded exterior curved and inviting. This is the kind of door that beckons, almost compels the desire to open and explore what lies beyond it. If you can see yourself walking up to the door, running your palms along its smoothness, inhaling the scent of an inviting fragrance that wafts through from the other side, then you have an idea of its mysterious attraction. There is a small, brass sign on the door, one word, simply lettered, "Wholeness."

It's impossible not to turn the knob and pull gently, although you somehow already know it will be locked. And in noticing this, you begin to question. The healing journey often starts this way, with a question. How did I get this disease? What will relieve my pain? Who am I? Will I ever be happy? Such questions are especially potent when accompanied by the raw shock of a newly diagnosed condition, or the vulnerability of some other life crisis. The world has turned upside down. It is at these times that we are most open to the possibility that our old assumptions and beliefs are incomplete and need updating.

The closed mechanistic view of Newtonian physics is still the basis for how conventional Western medicine is practiced today. This system is primarily concerned with curing the symptoms of disease and discomfort that affect the physical body. The concept of wholeness is entirely absent. It is all too easy to forget that the human system has its own wisdom and ability to ward off disease. We become focused on symptoms management, not understanding that true health and healing starts in the world within us.

The world within is the world of energy, feelings, and thought, of the greater part of you that is connected to Spiritual Intelligence. It contains infinite possibilities, infinite wisdom and power. There is a direct communication link from Spiritual Intelligence to your physical reality. It is called the central nervous system, and it includes the brain. *The nervous system is the translator of communication between the greater part of you (Spiritual Intelligence) and your physical reality.* This is an open system, continually transmitting information back and forth, continually creating the opportunity for healing. Even conventional Western medicine concedes that the largest and most efficient drug store is located in the brain and body. These biologically produced chemicals are totally natural, carry no side effects, and are balanced perfectly for the need at hand. In other words, your body is naturally self-healing and self-regulating.

When there is a block or interference in the nervous system, communication with the greater part of you is cut off. You have lost access to your inner healer, and you are at risk for illness and disease. A block in your innate ability to heal yourself may be caused by physical, mental, emotional, and spiritual stresses, injuries or toxicities. Because we are energetic beings and our physical body is part of a holistic energetic system, a traumatic emotional injury that is never healed can turn up in the form of a cancer years later.

Many people come to a Creative Self-Health orientation because they are living with a physical illness or disorder that conventional medicine has failed to help them resolve. Something tells them there has to be more to healing than what they've been told. They are no longer willing to passively accept the limitations of that old model for health.

Self-Health practices are based on the truth about health and healing. When you choose the Creative Self-Health journey, you make an active commitment to align with your inner healer. You will unlock the door to your wholeness, and step into a new vision for what is possible.

OH HEALING ENERGY

Oh healing energy flowing all through me
Oh healing energy flowing all through me

Oh healing energy
Take away my pain, take away my tears
Take away my sadness, take away my fears
And set me free

Oh healing energy flowing all through me
Oh healing energy flowing all through me

Oh healing energy
Open up my heart, fill it up with joy
Open up my heart, fill it up with love
And bring me peace

Oh healing energy flowing all through me
Oh healing energy flowing all through me

Oh healing energy
Reconnect my soul, turning on the light of life
Reconnect my soul, awakening my spirit
And make me whole again

Amen.

-Lori-Ann Gertonson

CHAPTER TWO

The Nervous System as Inner Healer

"Tension is who you think you should be.
Relaxation is who you are."
-Chinese Proverb

A healthy functioning nervous system opens the door to wholeness. Our brain and nerves conduct vitality back and forth from Spiritual Intelligence to our energetic and physical selves. The nervous system is a beautiful part of our inner healer, designed both to ensure physical survival and to optimize healthy living-the sympathetic system responds to tension or danger, while the parasympathetic system supports optimal living when we are relaxed.

In order to understand our Self-Health orientation,

we must understand how lifestyle and unhealed trauma produce the chronic tension that leads to disturbance in the flow of energy through the nervous system. Stress is the source of most of the tension we experience today. But what exactly is stress, and how does the nervous system react to it?

Stressing Out (of Alignment)

Most of us would say that life in the twenty-first century is filled with stresses that arise from work, family life, deadlines, financial worries. Stress is commonly thought of as a negative emotional state. However, it's important to know that stress is actually anything that results in a change to our biological system, whether positive or negative.

Exercise is an example of positive stress; it changes our system by adding muscle strength. Alternately, negative stress causes change that the body interprets as a threat to our survival. Negative stress includes the usual suspects- worry, guilt, fear, and anger-but it also includes biochemical stress from poor nutrition, drug use (prescribed or not), and physical stress from lack of exercise, repetitive motion injuries, and other trauma.

Flipping the Circuit Breakers on Stress

Let's look a little more closely at how negative stress disconnects us from our inner healer and leads to chronic health problems. The body is hard-wired to improve our chances of surviving emergencies. When the body interprets something as a threat, our fight/flight (sometimes referred to as fight/flight/freeze) response is activated, even when the "threat" is simply a bad feeling. This acute stress response from the sympathetic nervous system gives us the physical means to either fight-confront the threat, or flee-avoid the threat. Heart rate and blood pressure increase so more energy is sent to the extremities to help us run faster and jump higher. At the same time, this response supports our ability to be more alert-think faster, focus more intensely. Other systems, such as digestion, slow down. It is not important to eat lunch if you are about to be lunch! Even the immune system is temporarily slowed down. Blood vessels under the surface of the skin close down to minimize bleeding. The same physiology is in play with a freeze response, with internal hyper vigilance amped up as the body instinctively "plays dead" in order to trick the predator into leaving it alone.

When the human system is in balance a healthy

fight/flight/freeze response is short acting-once the danger has passed we rest, slow down, and recover. The parasympathetic part of our nervous system is then activated so we can heal our wounds and restore our energy. Today, most of the perceived threats that activate our fight/flight/freeze response are negative emotional experiences. The response is activated, but we can't act on it. We can't mount an attack, or run away, or even completely release the hyper-vigilant state. So, the body does not get the all-clear signal it needs to begin the recovery process. The acute stress response is prolonged and we don't get the opportunity to recover, rest, and restore ourselves. Additionally, most of these negative emotional states are triggered by unconscious thoughts-we are not aware of the thoughts, patterns, and limiting beliefs that cause the worry, fear, anger, and other stressors. The brain and entire nervous system is impacted, causing blocks and interferences in the vital flow of communication coming from Spiritual Intelligence.

On the physical level, prolonging our acute stress response is not sustainable. Stress hormones build up and chronic illness becomes more likely as the effects accumulate and our reserves become depleted.

Imagine a house full of appliances and computer systems all plugged into the electrical system. If the electrical circuits become overloaded, then the circuit breakers flip. Those circuit breakers are there to regulate and alter the flow of energy through your house, protecting the house from the worst effects of the electrical overload. When the energetic current through the electrical circuits is more than the system can handle, the circuits flip off automatically.

This is essentially what your body does under chronic stress. When suffering from chronic stress, your body's goal is not to be healthy and vital, but rather to survive. It adapts by establishing a new normal. It creates some physical misalignments (blocks and interferences in the nervous system) to alter the flow of energy and protect your body from overwhelm. Being chronically stressed means the nervous system normalizes a condition we were never meant to sustain, and over time the body begins to break down under the strain. When chronic stress is our normal state, the body systems are functioning in emergency mode even though we do not necessarily feel stressed. The natural flow of health and vitality becomes blocked and can't get through in this high stress level state. The inner healer cannot do its work. Since the condition now *feels* normal, we can easily miss the warning signs that the body is unable to cope until we are shocked by a diagnosis or illness that changes our perspective.

If we want to keep our circuits from overloading before illness strikes, we've got to unplug from the sources of stress. We start to unplug by calming the mind and relaxing the body.

The Other Side of Survival

If mental/emotional stress could be distilled into its two most simple forms, they would be worry about the future and pain from the past.

Remarkably, human beings are the only species known to respond to stresses that are not present in the moment. Because we can store thoughts and memories, we can also bring up memories of the past and relive them in the present. If the memory brings with it a stress response we feel that response as if the event were happening now. Likewise, we can think of or anticipate future stresses that haven't happened yet and with those thoughts bring about biochemical reactions in the body that produce a stress response without the stressful event actually occurring. The stress cycle is activated by thoughts, memories, and anticipation of unwanted outcomes. Because many of our mental and emotional stresses are stored in our unconscious mind, we are not always aware we are having stressful thoughts; we aren't aware the body is responding to unconscious negative thought patterns and beliefs.

Later in the book we will delve deeply into how these negative beliefs and patterns develop, as well as how we can eliminate them from our lives, but for now it's most important to note that the negative beliefs can be a source of chronic stress even when all else in our lives seems to be going smoothly. Now consider what life is like when the mental/emotional stress is compounded by a fast food diet and physical stress due to overwork, injury, or not getting enough sleep. Finally, add in the biochemical stress of taking pain and sleeping pills to relieve the symptoms of this lifestyle. This is the high stress norm that many of us call everyday life; we have become stuck in survival mode living. Survival mode living is tense living. It involves tight muscles, negative emotions and mental strain due to ongoing fight/flight response patterns. Remember, it is our inability to recover from that fight/flight stress response that depresses the immune system and eventually causes illness. Is it any wonder that chronic disease is so prevalent in today's world? Getting out of the high stress norm means getting unstuck from survival mode and back into recovery, calm, and balance. Although we are not yet directly addressing what caused the overload, we are moving into repair and healing mode. The activities that create calm turn the immune functions back on and support digestion and other functions that support growth, repair, and healing. The entire nervous system becomes nourished and renewed. The first step toward Self-Health is releasing the high-stress state, then we can begin to recreate health, and reconnect to Spiritual Intelligence.

Once you are on the other side of survival, healthy lifestyle choices can begin to support your growth and healing. This does not mean that life will never again present us with challenges or upsets, but rather when the nervous system is restored to its healthy balance and no longer stuck in survival mode, it has the ability to respond to emergencies. The healthy brain and nervous system reconnect to Spiritual Intelligence, reactivating the inner healer. Regular chiropractic care is a great way to keep the nervous system healthy. Chiropractors are nervous system experts, whose work is based on restoring the innate ability of the body to heal with Spiritual Intelligence. You can also make a commitment to your own self-care practices that activate the inner healer. If you are already taking responsibility for daily practices that calm and relax your system, great! If not, below are some suggestions you might try.

Getting Started

It's easier than you may think to start the process of calming the mind and relaxing the body. There are probably a few things you are already doing that support your de-stressing process. Exercise can use energy stored up from stress overload and release feel good endorphins in the body. Art, knitting, and Qigong are all wonderful ways to support the nervous system through focused activity. The key here is that whatever you are doing brings your focus and concentration to the present moment. This is important because being relaxed and present in the moment signals the brain and nervous system to begin healing, and starts the process of deepening your connection to Spiritual Intelligence.

The first thing to determine when you begin is what will work for you-what tools for de-stressing can be built into your daily life.

Recommended Self-Health Tool: Daily Meditation

We recommend developing a daily meditation practice as the single most effective calming strategy available. It can be hard to connect with your Spiritual Intelligence when you've spent years in high stress survival mode. The voices of stress speak loudly, while the intelligence within whispers. Meditation is the art of quieting your system down enough to begin to hear the whispers of the wise inner self.

Meditation is an ancient practice that has been scientifically validated in study after study. Meditation builds present moment focus skills like nothing else. By concentrating on a particular point of focus such as the breath for a specific period of time, you bring yourself to a place of calm and relaxation. Remembering to take even a single deep breath during a moment of stress can do wonders to bring clarity and calm into the situation, so intentionally focusing on the breath in meditation can do a lot for you over time. Just a few of the benefits of regular meditation include:

- Reduction in stress and anxiety
- Increased creativity
- Lowered blood pressure
- Greater sense of calm and wellbeing
- Improved concentration
- Deepening self awareness

Meditation affects the central nervous system (which includes the brain) in very specific ways to bring about these benefits. In everyday life, the brain is producing waves of different frequencies as needed for different types of situations. For instance, beta waves are most commonly associated with normal daily tasks. Your conscious mind is making sense of the world and its stimuli with beta waves. In stressful situations, beta waves are activated at high levels.

Alpha waves are produced when you are relaxed. This is the state that begins to penetrate into the realm of the subconscious, allowing access to information and awareness that are not found when you are externally focused. As you've probably guessed, a light meditative state is an alpha state. This is also the state where the body begins to deactivate its fight/flight response.

Deep meditation produces theta waves, a state that can seem trance-like and penetrates even more deeply into the subconscious mind than alpha waves. Delta waves are even slower than theta waves and are associated with deep sleep.

With regular meditation practice, you give your body the chance to restore itself and recover from high stress, you tap into the subconscious mind where old negative beliefs can be eliminated, and you develop the skill to regulate your brain wave patterns.

Choices in Meditation

Once you've decided meditation is for you, it can be confusing to figure out which type of meditation is best. For instance, some people will be drawn to traditional sitting meditation, while others find a movement-oriented meditation such as mindful walking more appealing. Either way, beginners often bring certain expectations to meditation that can hinder their progress. One of our favorite friends and meditation teachers, Sarah Lewis, would often compare learning to meditate to house training a puppy. When you first put the puppy (your thoughts) on the paper, it won't understand what you want and it will quickly wander off. It takes time and patience to continually bring the puppy back to the paper. Gradually, with practice, the puppy starts to realize what is wanted and begins to go to the paper by herself. Training your mind to meditate works in a similar fashion. Kindness, patience, and commitment are key factors.

It's important to know that it may take time to try out several types of meditative methods before you find the one that suits you. You may even develop a wonderful practice that serves you for a number of months or years and then find yourself drawn to a different method. Other ways to learn about meditation include reading books, taking classes or listening to YouTube videos.

Recommended Self-Health Tool: Take a Breather!

Using the breath as a point of focus is common, mainly because the breath is always available. You can be standing in line or sitting at work and still find a few seconds to calm yourself by focusing on the breath. For more formal daily practice, here's one way to begin: Find a time when you will not be disturbed or interrupted for five to fifteen minutes. Be sure to turn off your cell phone and any other noisy distractions. Sit comfortably with your eyes closed. Begin to focus your attention on your breath. You can focus on the point of entry of breath at your nostrils or the movement of breath into your belly. Notice all you can about the flow of breath into and out of your body, and when you find yourself being distracted by thoughts or physical discomfort simply return your attention to the breath. Continue doing this for at least five minutes. Congratulations! You've just meditated. Do this practice every day, gradually lengthening the amount of time you spend, up to fifteen minutes.

Things to Remember:

Negative stress-Stress is not just a bad feeling. It comes from physical, emotional, mental, and biochemical sources.

Activate Your Inner Healer-Calming the mind and relaxing the body support your ability to heal the effects of stress overload and balance your system. Chiropractic adjustments support self-regulation and self-healing as well as the release of physical and emotional trauma.

Make De-stressing a habit-Discover the tools for de-stressing that work for you, and build them into your daily life.

Meditate Regularly-A daily meditation practice is the gold standard for calming the mind and body. Building a meditation practice takes time and commitment, but the resulting payoffs are well worth it. The deeper the state of meditation, the easier it is to connect to Spiritual Intelligence.

CHAPTER THREE

The Spiritually Intelligent Heart

"My heart knows what my mind only thinks it knows."

-Noah Benshea

What if your thoughts are just distractions, yelling over the whispers of your heart?

If you could communicate with Spiritual Intelligence, the greater part of you that houses your wholeness,, what would you say? Would you have questions, requests, or complaints? Would you be willing to listen as this Intelligence replied? Even if you had to learn a new way of listening in order to really hear? Would you be willing to be guided by the whispers from the heart of your very being?

Accessing the wisdom of Spiritual Intelligence from within means we choose to listen to the heartfelt whisper that is the source of love, creativity and health. This is not always easy. Most of us have at least some limiting beliefs we live by that cause us mental and emotional stress. We have struggled with feelings and/or thoughts that tell us we are unworthy, unlovable, incapable. These thoughts and feelings are often persistent and persuasive. When we believe them, we suffer. Our guidance from Spiritual Intelligence becomes blocked, and our ability to make healthy choices is diminished. Releasing limiting beliefs can restore the flow of heartfelt communication to and from Spiritual Intelligence. In order to do that, it helps to understand how limiting beliefs are formed and why they are so ingrained.

Imagine a park in the middle of a busy city. A lot of people from the neighborhood go walking in the park, and over time a natural path has been worn into the grass and dirt from so many footsteps. Whenever a newcomer visits the park, she will automatically tend to follow the path that has already been worn into the ground.

In this same way, our brains have been impacted by old beliefs firing along the same neural pathways over the years. As they are triggered over and over again, the primary neural pathways form a type of highly efficient super highway, called a neural net. Neural net patterns establish our habitual ways of seeing and understanding. We make life choices based on these habitual patterns, even when the pattern results in stress and disconnect from Spiritual Intelligence.

Experience Influences Belief

Everett has long gray hair and rides a bike to his job as a lifeguard at the local pool. An athletic and vigorous man, he describes himself as "an old jock" in a deep gravelly voice that attracts attention wherever he goes.

Still, with the approach of his seventieth birthday, he'd been feeling the weight of this milestone and troubled by the thought that his best years were behind him. He recalled that as a boy he loved to watch the annual parade held by his hometown, anticipating the day he would be an adult marching along with all the others. For years, young Everett took in every detail of the event with great excitement, including the audience of older men sitting on the sidelines as the parade marched past. Now, as Everett began to grapple with his anxiety and grief about getting older, he realized that the image he'd seen at the parade had lodged in his child-mind as a belief that the place for older men was in the background, watching but not participating in all the action of life.

The belief was the source of his sadness, telling him that at seventy his life options were now severely limited, and that he did not have much to contribute anymore. In discovering how the belief was shaping his understanding of aging, Everett was able to question the truth of his childhood experience. Elation and relief filled him as he realized he was still able to march in the parade, but that now he had earned the right to march at his own pace. He returned to training as a competitive swimmer, and even began to participate in races.

Most beliefs develop out of experience, particularly childhood experiences, like the one young Everett had watching the parade. Since young children are sensitive and open beings who do not understand how and why the world works, they are often confused or traumatized by life experiences. Traumatic and confusing experiences influence the child to form protective beliefs that are erroneous. This is a brilliant defense system, whose purpose is to allow the child to survive the overwhelming experience. However, once formed the belief is stored for years in the unconscious, unseen but powerful, where it continues to distort even adult perceptions.

For all its difficulties, the ability to store beliefs out of conscious awareness is important and necessary. For example, when we touch a hot stove we feel the pain of that and register a belief-it's best not to touch hot stoves. We can now rely on that information and simply avoid touching hot stoves in the future, without having to think through or revisit the painful experience. We could not live very efficiently without this ability to establish a belief system about how the world works and live within its parameters. Safety and ease are real benefits to this ability.

At the same time, young children do not have the capacity to always correctly interpret events and situations. Even positive events, like the parade for young Everett, may carry unconscious associations that are ultimately limiting. So this ability is also the source of limiting beliefs formed through ignorance, confusion, or trauma.

Belief Defines Experience

As children, we primarily experience the world through our five senses. External events, our environment, and the people surrounding us all contribute to our perceptions. The very nature of childhood, with its inherent vulnerability, underlies the need to create protective beliefs systems. While many of these beliefs serve us very well, each of us also carries within a set of beliefs that started out as protective, but now limit our health and happiness. By the time we have grown into adulthood, our brains have been trained to automatically perceive and sort for truth based on the unconscious limiting belief systems formed in childhood. Since most of this belief-making action is taking place at an unconscious level, we don't notice it. Our pre-programmed brain is set up to lead us back to the same conclusions over and over again. It does not let in the awareness of new evidence to challenge the old beliefs. This loop in the brain has shut down the flow of information from Spiritual Intelligence.

For example, if the belief is "I am incompetent", every positive event such as a promotion based on work performance will be interpreted as "they just haven't seen my incompetence yet, but they'll find out and when they do I'll be fired". This is sadly the way many people spend their whole life, trying to cope with the pain and doubt caused by limiting beliefs and the problems they cause. The good news is that when such a problem arises it gives us the opportunity to release beliefs that are not serving us.

If Everett had never questioned his belief that life was essentially over at seventy, he could easily have sunk into depression and become one of the old men on the sidelines of life. His limiting belief would have been fulfilled, despite the fact that he was still capable of participating in his chosen sport. Instead, he discovered that although we can't stop the aging process, or many other events that are a part of life, we can release our limiting beliefs about these events and embrace a new, more supportive understanding of life. The release of limiting beliefs impacts our central nervous system as it allows us to make new neural connections and pathways. When the nervous system is aligned and unblocked, the flow of communication from Spiritual Intelligence and the larger aspects of our being are re-established. The whispers from the intelligence within can be heard more clearly, and we are free to experience ourselves beyond the limits of our belief systems. Our power to create a vital, joy-filled life has been restored.

The Release Process

The process of releasing limiting beliefs can be divided into four stages, which do not necessarily proceed in a linear fashion toward release, but rather support and enhance each other, as new information is integrated into the individual's worldview.

The first stage of the process is recognition. What is unconscious is unseen. Like the fish that does not recognize water, our belief systems are so much a part of our world that we are unaware of the great impact they have. Chronic conditions, recurring problems, behavioral patterns, and feeling stuck are clues that a limiting belief is active. It's important to approach recognition with some patience. Some beliefs will show themselves rather readily as we begin to listen to ourselves speak and watch our own actions. But other beliefs may require the assistance of friends or professionals in order to unearth them. Once a belief has been identified, the next stage is questioning the validity of the belief. This requires a great deal of self-honesty and compassion. The third stage is willingness. This means being willing to release the old belief and feel the emotions associated with letting go of the familiar. Finally, we enter the stage of Creative Self-Health. Here we become active participants in creating a new worldview, one born from our restored connection with Spiritual Intelligence.

Recommended Self-Health Tool: Meditation

Continuing the meditation practice started in chapter two also provides another benefit for the release process. Regular meditation develops what is known as a Witness Consciousness. The Witness is the part of you that observes the self without judgment, including your own thoughts and behavioral patterns. When you meditate you begin to notice your thoughts without getting distracted by them, and when you are in a deeply relaxed state, your unconscious thoughts are more likely to surface. This is great support for recognition, the first stage of the release process.

Recommended Self-Health Tool: Inquiry

Once a belief has been identified, it is extremely important to notice all we can about the habitual patterns of the belief. Gentle inquiry is a way of questioning our thoughts. A question asked in this manner with a friendly sort of curiosity provides us with valuable information about the belief. Some sample questions around beliefs might be:

- When did I develop this belief?
- How do I know it's true?
- What else might explain the events that happened around this belief?
- What else might be true that I don't usually think about this belief?

When asking these questions in a gentle, patient

way, it is common to experience feelings like anger, grief, shame, and fear. It is crucial to have a support system in place to help navigate these feelings.

Recommended Self-Health Tool: Forgiveness

Uncovering the emotions of old trauma and the beliefs that come from trauma require healing the wounded heart. In Creative Self-Health practice, forgiveness is the act of letting go of the painful past and returning to the peace of connection with Spiritual Intelligence. Forgiveness does not excuse or condone harmful acts. It does not make what happened okay. True forgiveness acknowledges all the pain and suffering of our past experience without letting that pain continue to hurt us in the present. It honors both our human experience of pain and suffering, and the wider spiritual perspective on life events.

While forgiveness cannot be forced, a good place to start is to notice if there is a willingness to forgive. As in the release of limiting beliefs, willingness is the foundation for transformative change. Often, unwillingness to forgive indicates a belief that forgiveness is condoning the harmful act or behavior. If that is the case, it is important to accept and explore that belief, as in the inquiry process above.

- Am I willing to forgive?
- If not, what does forgiveness mean to me?
- If yes, what does forgiveness mean to me?
- Am I willing to let go of this pain and suffering?
- If not, what need is being met by my pain?

It may take a long time to develop willingness, or not much time at all. Each individual will have a unique timeline for this preparation period, depending on the severity of the harmful event and many other factors. Sometimes we have to start with being willing to be willing! What matters is that we start with wherever we are. Once willingness is established, the next step is acknowledgement. This is the telling of what happened and all the ways it affected you. This step includes all the emotions and beliefs that came out of that experience. It is a tender process, often needing support and witnessing by a trusted friend or professional. Next, look again at the beliefs surrounding the experience, and inquire into the truth of those beliefs. Here again, having a support system in place is crucial. People often blame themselves (sometimes unconsciously) for negative events and crises. Questioning these beliefs with compassion for self restores peace of mind and heart. There is always another way to see and define experience. Forgiveness asks us to bring new meaning to our most difficult experiences. For some, that meaning is found in inspiration and acting to prevent others from going through what we've gone through. For others, integrating the experience as a spiritual lesson, perhaps only understandable from a soul level, is healing. The meaning is only discovered in the process, by making the commitment to one's own peace of mind and heart. Finally, the last stage in the forgiveness process is gratitude. Gratitude is another exercise in present moment awareness. We express gratitude for the gifts gained from the opportunity to go through the forgiveness process. Compassion, peace, acceptance, and equanimity are just a few of the gifts that are often found as we forgive. When gratitude is added to these gifts, it opens the door to joy.

Recommended Self-Health Tool: Gratitude

We recommend gratitude as a powerful practice both combined with forgiveness and as a stand-alone exercise. Practicing gratitude brings attention to what is positive about the present. When practiced in a heartfelt way, it is not just a mental exercise, but it is accompanied by deep feelings and healthy biochemical responses in the body. Gratitude practice can start as simply as keeping a journal where you note what you are grateful for at the end of each day. Finding something positive to focus on and sitting with it until the feeling fills your heart promotes health and vitality. Another practice is writing a letter to someone you appreciate, even if that person has passed away. Lori-Ann recalls a most difficult time in her life, when her parents had passed away within weeks of each other. She had spent months flying back and forth across the country tending to her parents at one end and her own young family and career at the other. At last, while still on the east coast, and saddened by the latest funeral, Lori chose to do a gratitude practice. She bought a card and sat down with a cup of tea. She began to write about all she had learned and discovered in the midst of her loss. As she wrote she allowed herself to feel deeply each lesson, and every blessing she had encountered during her months of caregiving. Then, she put the card in an envelope and mailed it to herself at her address in California. Shortly after she returned home, the card arrived, giving her another experience of the great comfort and joy she had found during this challenging time.

Recommended Self-Health Tool: Affirmation

Oftentimes when a limiting belief is released the process itself opens up a fresh way of seeing. Affirmations are positive statements that express a new perspective. They can be simple, such as "I am worthy". The key to using affirmations is the same as with gratitude practice, the statement must move beyond just expressing a nice thought. It requires a depth of emotion that brings life to the words. The affirmation must be felt with the heart in order for it to be effective. To make this easier, pick a person you love dearly. Picture that person in your mind. Now feel that person in your heart. Allow your love for that person to fill your heart. Now affirm aloud, "She is worthy." Feel the truth of the affirmation and the appreciation you have for that person. Now gently let your attention move to yourself. Bring yourself into your own heart in the same manner, and allow the same emotions to fill your heart as you do. Now affirm aloud, "I am worthy." It's okay if you do not feel the same depth of emotion for yourself as you do for another. Each time you practice with affirmations you will become more willing to open your heart to yourself as well as to others. The most powerful affirmations will come out of your discovery process as you release your limiting beliefs. But a few sample affirmations might include:

- I am worthy
- I love myself unconditionally
- I accept myself as I am
- I eat healthy nutritious foods
- I embrace abundance in all aspects of my life

Notice that every affirmation is said in the present tense, not as something that will happen in the future. There are many resources for and examples of affirmations in books and online. As with all practices, consistency is key. Start gradually with one or two affirmations that particularly draw you.

Things to Remember:

Limiting Beliefs-Limiting beliefs stored in the unconscious disconnect us from Spiritual Intelligence and hold us back from living full and balanced lives. Releasing limiting beliefs is a transformative process. A support system of friends, community, and/or professionals is essential. An added benefit of meditation is that it helps us to get in touch with unconscious limiting beliefs. Practices of forgiveness, gratitude, and daily affirmations are all part of creating a new, healthy worldview. Below the noise of limiting thoughts, whispers from the Spiritually Intelligent heart are always available.

Heartfelt Thanks

For all mothers, fathers, sisters, and brothers

For all spouses, sons and daughters

For all grandmothers and grandfathers

For all friends, teachers and healers

For all those who have touched our lives

    Heartfelt Thanks

For the fish in the sea and the birds in the sky

For all flowers, plants and tress

For the air we breathe and the rain that falls

For all that nourishes us

    Heartfelt Thanks

For mother earth, from the mountains to the oceans

For the sun, the moon and the stars

For the planets, galaxies, and the universe

For all creation and its gifts to us all

    Heartfelt Thanks

For all the love given and received

    Heartfelt Thanks

For the special gift of you in my life

    Heartfelt Thanks   -Lori-Ann   Gertonson

CHAPTER FOUR

Choosing Vitality

"Lasting change cannot occur without transformation of the heart."
-Nathan W. Morris

Look into the eyes of a ninety-year-old woman who is happy, active, strong, and mentally aware. There is a quality of being shining from within, a sense of vitality that comes with full immersion in life and all it has to offer. Vitality is a gift from Spiritual Intelligence that is offered to us throughout our lifetime. It exists independent of age and even physical ability, yet the lifestyle choices we make will determine whether vitality will expand or diminish with time. When it is given what it needs, the body is a self-healing and self-regulating system that functions perfectly as a vehicle for the vital expression of life.

Vitality comes from the nourishment of mind, body, and spirit. It is a dynamic quality, moving and changing with each life stage. It is critically responsive to how we care for ourselves physically, yet is sourced in our mental, emotional and spiritual aspects. Vitality is one of the hallmarks of connection with Spiritual Intelligence.

Would You Rather be Healthy or Just Not Sick?

Most of us weren't brought up to consider vitality as a lifestyle choice. Our cultural orientation tells us that if we have no overt symptoms of illness we are well. The annual physical at the doctor's office consists of a series of tests to make sure no signs of illness are present, but how often is a discussion of optimal nutrition or emotional wellbeing a part of the exam? Prevention is about staving off illness rather than promoting vitality and wholeness. If an illness or symptom is found, it is likely treated with a prescription drug designed to return you to a state of not sick, or at least not symptomatic. This "not-sick" state is deemed normal in today's world and often called healthy. But if we look closely at the states of sick and not sick, then compare them to vitality, the difference fairly leaps out at us. If you had a pair of shoes that didn't fit, the discomfort might be such that you'd take the shoes off. Being barefoot certainly feels better than wearing ill-fitting shoes, but is not the same as having the perfect pair of shoes that are comfortable, supportive, attractive and fit well. Just as you would still have to go out and find the shoes that truly fit, it is clear that something more is needed in order to move from not sick to vitality. Sometimes an illness or chronic condition acts as a catalyst that compels us to explore and redefine what health is, giving us the motivation to learn the difference between sick, not sick, and vitality. Vitality encompasses the larger aspects of our being along with the physical body, including a fully functioning connection with Spiritual Intelligence.

Like any lifestyle, choosing vitality is an ongoing process. It usually involves letting go of some habits and patterns that do not enhance health and wholeness, and making new choices that do. This choice making is taking place at every moment of your life, and each choice is leading you toward or away from vitality. In this chapter we will take a look at some essentials that foster vitality, and explore the secrets of vital aging.

Essentials of Vitality

There are four broad areas where lifestyle choices can be made to support vitality. They are nourishment, movement, relationship, and community. Of course, these areas overlap and intertwine, each enhancing the others. As we move from a not-sick orientation toward choosing vitality, our understanding of each area widens, and our experience of them deepens. We find that spiritual connectivity informs each area, and that vitality is strengthened as our connection with Spiritual Intelligence grows.

Nourishment

Food is a struggle for many of us. Fraught with guilt and shame about weight, or frustrated with conflicting information on how, what, and when to eat, it might be easier if we could just go cold turkey and quit, but that's not an option. So when speaking of diet, there is a tendency to be drawn back into this sense of the difficulty with food. Instead, we invite you to take a deep breath, refocus, and notice what you can feel about the possibility of being deeply nourished. Consider the question, what is nourishment? There is nourishment of body, mind, and spirit. How would it feel to be nourished by the aromas of fresh food as the flavor dissolves on your tongue and sends strength to your every organ; to awaken relaxed and restored from a deeply restful sleep of many hours; to quench your thirst with a glass of pure spring water on a hot day; or to enjoy your favorite music with your best friend by your side? Nourishment is a form of healthy self-love. As you read further, we invite you to stop periodically and remind yourself that the purpose of eating well is nourishment.

Aligning with Your Design

We are designed to eat well. Our bodies need nutrient rich food sources in order to express the energy of life. We were created to consistently eat moderate amounts of these nutrient rich foods in order to have a healthy weight, high energy, and be resistant to illness and disease. Aligning with the way your body was designed to be nourished by food is complicated by fast food culture, soil depletion, polluted waters, and the treatment of feed animals. The result is a population of overweight and malnourished people. Because of the way food has been industrialized and farmed over the years, it's not as easy to get access to the full range of nutrients our bodies need. We are intimately connected with our ecosystem. When we eat a steak that comes from a hormone treated, grain-fed cow, the biochemical result in our bodies is the same as if we had eaten the grains or taken the hormones ourselves. In the same way, polluted water and pesticides absorbed by the plants we ingest become a part of our human system. How, then, can we be assured that we are supplied with the nutritional support our bodies need in order to function well? The answer is to replicate as closely as possible the life-sustaining diet for which our bodies were originally designed.

Luckily, much research has already been done that tells us exactly how the body is designed and what it needs to thrive. One of the most nourishing system for eating we've come across is a pH balanced diet.

In her book, *The Ultimate pH Solution*, Michelle Schoffro Cook explains that your pH level is the balance between acid and alkaline in your blood. The standard American diet and lifestyle causes the body to become dangerously acidic, upsetting the normal pH balance. Acid overload is the precursor to a number of diseases including diabetes, depression, osteoporosis, and weight problems. Foods such as sugar, white flour, grains and dairy are acidic. Environmental toxins and stress also cause the blood to become acidic. If you've guessed that fresh, organic vegetables are alkalizing you are correct. In fact, optimally we were designed to eat a diet that is 70-75% vegetables and fruit, and 25-30% protein (from either vegetable or non-toxic animal sources). Cook's book outlines the science behind acid overload and gives clear guidelines on how to make alkalizing food and lifestyle choices. Unfortunately, health conscious eaters need to be aware that because of agricultural practices and environmental toxins, the amount of nutrition available in a cup of spinach today is far less than that which was available from the same cup in our grandmother's time. We simply cannot eat enough healthy foods to make up for the nutritional value that has been lost. Supplements are crucial to fill the nutritional gap left by the state of our food supply and to compensate for the impact of stressful living on our immune systems. In fact, the term "supplements" is a bit misleading, since they are in essence now a part of eating well. So what supplements are must haves on your grocery list?

Probiotics-Before agriculture became big business, we ate plants that came from soil rich in certain bacteria that support human life. These bacteria digest the fibrous parts of plants that we cannot. The byproducts of that digestive process are important vitamins, especially the B vitamins. Now, the natural symbiotic (mutually supportive) relationship between these bacteria and humans has been disrupted by changes in the way our foods are farmed and brought to us. We depend more on grains than plants to supply the B vitamins we need, but the digestion of so many grains results in a more acidic physical environment, offsetting any benefits we may experience from the vitamins. Taking a probiotic supplement supports the digestive process and a whole lot more, since the digestive system is centrally linked to maintaining optimal immune function and nourishing the nervous system.

Prebiotics-It is becoming more common to supplement with prebiotics, however the simple truth is prebiotics are just plant foods containing indigestible (by people) fiber that feed the probiotics. As recommended above, eating a diet of at least 70-75% vegetables and some fruit will not only keep your body alkalized, supplied with minerals, but will also maintain a healthy microbiome. Eating a variety of vegetables will likely provide the necessary prebiotics needed by the different gut bacteria.

Multivitamins-High quality food-based multivitamins provide the extra nutrients to help us cope with environmental toxins and stressors, and to make up for the deficiencies of even a healthy modern diet. This type of multivitamin is not found on the typical drug store counter, and does not contain artificial binders and synthetics. The multivitamins we recommend are food-based, pre digested by our friendly bacteria, and highly absorbable.

Healthy Fats (Omega 3 fats)-Certain kinds of healthy fat are needed to combat inflammation and support cell structure and function in every part of the body, especially brain cells in our nervous system. Omega 3 and Omega 6 fats are healthy nutrients called essential fatty acids .The average American diet is dangerously low in Omega 3 fats, and high in Omega 6 fats found in grains such as corn and wheat. This imbalance sets the stage for many disease processes. Originally we were supposed to get Omega 3 fats from grass-eating wild game, fish, or plant based vegetables, nuts and seeds. Supplementing with Omega 3 fats and choosing to eat the meat of pasture-raised grass-fed animals is recommended to restore this critical balance. Wild oily fishes such as salmon and sardines, while still a good source of Omega 3 fats, must be consumed in limited amounts due to the state of toxic pollution in our water. We do more harm than good for our bodies by consuming the typically grain-fed animals and mercury containing fish that are readily available today.

Antioxidant Superfoods- Stress is an all too familiar presence in our everyday lives. But did you know that we are stressed not just from mental and emotional turmoil, but from eating acidic foods? Further, we live in an environment that routinely exposes us to stress in the form of everything from x-rays to the electromagnetic frequencies produced by cell phones, computers, and even television sets. The more stress, the more free radicals are released in the body, causing damage to cells. Mental stress and eating poorly, plus an environment filled with toxins, all contribute to free radical damage to the cells. The cumulative effect of all this is called oxidative stress.

After the body has been at a high level of stress over a period of time, it adjusts to that high level of oxidative stress as normal, but loses its capacity to cope with more stress. A breakdown is occurring within, silent and unseen.

Think of oxidation in your cells as the same process that you see when metal rusts. If you leave your bike out in the rain, eventually it will begin to rust. When metal rusts the process is called oxidization. Free radicals are like the rain that causes oxidative stress, rusting us from the inside out, through aging and disease.

Anti-oxidant superfoods combat the oxidative process. They provide the dense nutrients needed to protect our bodies as we go about our daily business in our toxic, stress-filled twenty-first century world. They are also known as adaptogens, substances that help us adapt to biochemical and environmental changes, minimizing the effects of oxidative stress. They assist the body in coming back into natural balance instead of adopting high stress levels as the new normal that results in free radical damage.

Vitamin D3-There are few supplements that have been as thoroughly researched and proven valuable as vitamin D. It supports our bones, immune function, and heart. It helps prevent hypertension, cancer, and infectious diseases. Sunlight is the natural source of this essential vitamin, and it is often recommended that people get vitamin D from exposure to sun. But studies have shown that the vast majority of the population is dangerously deficient in vitamin D, mainly because unless you can spend thirty minutes or so everyday with most of your body exposed to sunlight (think bikini or shorts only) it is unlikely you are getting enough sun exposure for the amount of vitamin D needed. This is complicated by the fact that we are told to wear sunscreen to protect us from the dangers of ultra violet rays, which also means we are not getting the benefits of vitamin D from sunlight. Ironically, skin cancer rates are actually increasing with the use of sunscreen because it prevents us from absorbing enough vitamin D. (Note: We recommend that if you do decide to use sunscreen, choose one made from natural substances, so that you are not absorbing chemical toxins through your skin)

Other diets that have become popular recently include Paleo, Keto, Fodmap, and Autoimmune Protocol.

So what about Paleo and Keto diets?

Here is a brief overview of each.

A Paleo diet is based on the foods that were available in the wild to the early hunter-gatherer humans. It is what our digestive system was designed to eat. This would include fruits, vegetables, nuts, seeds fish, and meat and fats from wild animals. It was the diet of humans before agriculture was introduced and we became dependent on grains, and domesticated animals fed grains.

What about the Keto diet? The Keto or ketogenic diet is based on reducing the high carbohydrate, think grain and sugar, diet many have become accustomed to. It focuses on replacing these carbohydrates with fat. The premise is that by eating a diet of 70-75% fat, the body will burn the fat for energy and turn it into ketones, which can be used by the brain and body for energy. There have been many claims that the keto diet may provide many health benefits from weight loss to metabolic and insulin related diseases. While this may provide these benefits vs. the standard high carbohydrate diet, it is our opinion that based on the body's design, high fats may not have been the primary source of nourishment for early humans due to availability. We may be able to tolerate this diet, but it is our opinion that the Paleo diet is more in line with human design.

You may have heard of the Fodmap diet also. This is a diet designed to help people with irritable bowel syndrome and is not a recommended nutrition plan for everyone. It stands for Fermentable Oligo-Di-Mono-saccharides And Polyols. These are scientific words to describe the carbohydrates that may cause digestive symptoms.

Autoimmune Protocol Diet is a diet that has been developed to help people with a leaky gut and autoimmune diseases. Again this is a diet that is specific to people with chronic illness and not recommended nutrition plan. However, the basis for most of this diet is very similar to a Paleo diet.

There are many other "diets" to assist people with digestive illnesses, but it is our desire in this section to focus on what nourishes our body and allows vitality to be expressed fully.

Rest

Few things are as nourishing as a deep, restorative night's sleep. Negative stress, environmental toxins, biochemical imbalances, physical pain, and poor diet, all the very same culprits that deplete our nutritional status, can also affect our ability to sleep well. Recently, insomnia has been indicated as a cause of weight gain, adding to the list of problems caused by going without the good nightly rest we were designed to have.

Hydration

Dehydration is a silent epidemic in our society. We commonly reach for coffee, soda, tea, or even juice before plain water. Yet the average adult body is composed of 57-60% water, and needs a daily dose of at least half the body's weight in ounces of water to operate as designed. Some symptoms of chronic thirst include overeating (thirst signals from the body can often be confused as hunger), dark yellow urine, and constipation.

Intermittent Fasting

While it may seem counterintuitive, another nourishing practice that aligns with our design is intermittent fasting. Most of us in contemporary western society are eating every couple of hours. This would be considered feasting by the standards of our ancestors. Since our bodies were designed to withstand periods of famine, health is actually supported by not feasting all the time. Let's take a look at how this works through a simple equation. Food=Fuel=Energy. There are two types of fuel we can burn for energy. They are sugar and fat. Sugar is the fuel that the body accesses fastest and with the most ease. Most of us know by now that too much sugar is not good for the body and can lead to chronic illness. So relying solely on sugar as fuel is not the healthiest approach to a good energy source. The other source of fuel is fat. Fat is a better fuel to burn but our bodies don't access it readily because so much sugar is available through the typical western diet.

The solution is a practice called intermittent fasting. When we fast, we reduce our caloric intake in order to let the body get access to fat as a source of energy. This also helps reset our sugar metabolism, reducing our risk for chronic illnesses such as diabetes and even cancer. Other benefits include reducing inflammation, weight loss, and hormone balancing.

While we do not recommend intermittent fasting for people who are pregnant, breastfeeding, or have certain chronic illnesses, but for those who are healthy and have medical permission, there are a number of ways to do it. Some recommend eating only during certain hours of the day, such as 11:00 am to 7:00 pm, or reducing calories to 500-600 for one day per week. Our favorite method is the Isagenix nutritional cleansing system, which includes a full detoxification program along with the fast that has been proven by independent study to be more effective than a heart healthy diet. It is also worth noting that intermittent fasting has a long history as a spiritual practice in different traditions, and can be an avenue of directing conscious attention toward connection with Spiritual Intelligence.

Movement

Our hunter-gatherer ancestors were constantly on

the move. They used their bodies in all dimensions to lift, squat, run, jump, and reach in the course of their daily lives. Their muscles were worked naturally by the daily activities involved in the hunting and foraging for food. These well-worked muscles also maintained balance and stability so movement was efficient. Everyday life provided plenty of opportunity to move in the ways the human body was designed for, and to support physical health by doing so. There was no need to exercise in the way that we think of exercise today. Our modern work world tends to be focused on mental activities that create stress, while sitting for hours at a time, or moving in limited and repetitive ways. Recent studies, such as a report published in the January, 2015 Annals of Internal Medicine, have linked prolonged daily sitting with so many health hazards that sitting is now being touted as the new smoking! Inactivity has been linked to depression, diabetes, joint pain, heart disease, and the list goes on. Many injuries and illnesses are fostered by the lack of natural movement our lifestyles encourage. But like nourishment, movement has several qualities including and beyond the physical. Movement is the inhalation of the breath that pauses our distressing thoughts, the empathetic widening of our awareness to take in another's point of view, and the opening of our hearts in response. Movement is the flow aspect of vitality. We were designed as creatures of movement, adaptable to change, able to flex and stretch our capacities for life. Yet like every other ability, if we do not use movement in alignment with our design we pay a price in health and well -being. So dancing to music, playing sports, walking for pleasure, swimming laps, pulling weeds in the garden, squatting down to draw pictures in the sand, lifting a toddler into the air, and breathing deeply are all movements that honor our original design. Incorporating more and varied movement into our lives can be done in small steps, and does not depend on a gym membership or buying expensive equipment. What is the best exercise or movement program? THE ONE YOU WILL DO!!!! Whatever you like to do. And it is cumulative, so you do not have to do it all at once. In our stressful world, movement is one readily available way to help yourself to feel better. Movement will change your state. It will loosen your muscles, stimulate deep breathing, and burn off adrenaline and other harmful chemicals produced by stress.

Benefits of Regular Daily Movement

- A significant increase in your energy levels and stamina

- Higher state of general health and ideal weight
- Better muscle tone
- More enthusiasm and confidence
- Greater alertness and mental poise
- Less illness and enhanced productivity
- More discipline in all areas of your life
- Increased circulation and oxygenation
- Much greater resistance to stress
- Improved mood & better sleep
- Slows the aging process

These basic Self-Health lifestyle choices in nourishment and movement are foundational to vitality. Enjoying lifelong health and well-being can start at any age and continue as long as we live. And since many of us are likely to reach a ripe old age, it's worth exploring some specifics around aging with vitality.

Secrets to Vital Aging

Sixteen may be sweet, but there is no time of life riper with opportunities for self-reflection, spiritual growth, and meaningful relationship than after age forty. The stresses of mid-life are many, and the cultural pressure to defy aging is tremendous, yet the potential for vital aging offers gifts that cannot be found at any other stage of living. This is the time when maturity and vitality can combine to exponentially enhance our sense of gratitude for being alive, our understanding of what it is to be human, and our present moment awareness.

Vital aging is more challenging partly because there are so many caricatures of aging in popular western culture, and what is not seen as laughable is often pitied. Our fear of death and loss lie unexamined beneath these negative images. It's no wonder we don't want to look old, feel old, or be old. In fact, as we will discover in later chapters, our *beliefs* about aging (and any other condition) may determine more about our experience than anything else related to it.

In an article titled The Psychology of Aging and Longevity, Dr. Mario Martinez asserts that cultural context (what we believe as a culture about aging) determines our actual aging experiences. Dr. Martinez writes, "For example, while a sixty-two year old from an industrialized culture is engaged in behaviors conducive to achieving retirement, a Tarahumara Indian counterpart of the Chihuahua region of Mexico may be running up to 200 miles in a competitive racing sport called "kick ball" that can last several days. The Tarahumaras, known for their longevity, believe that growing older makes them stronger and consequently better runners. Retirement is not one of their bio-cultural portals. Interestingly, since the Tarahumaras look forward to their expected physical gains from growing older, "middle age crisis" is unknown to them and the usual degenerative pathology associated with aging is rare in their culture.

In our own culture, consider that people are living longer without necessarily living well. This is partially a reflection of chronic problems stemming from the limitations of the traditional medical care system, our nutrient-deficient food supply, and toxic environment. Add to this our sedentary culture. We spend a large part of our days sitting, whereas the culture and lifestyle of the Tarahumaras promotes activity."

Our western culture and media is permeated with negative bias against getting older, which creates among other things a sense of social isolation and lack of value in the elderly. It's a rather bleak picture of aging, isn't it? The good news is it doesn't have to be this way. In fact, YOU hold the key to healing and becoming more vital as you age. Almost everyone has heard of someone who is aging with grace, dignity, and purpose. If this seems to be the exception rather than the rule, it may have more to do with the fact that there are few examples of vital living at any age in western mainstream media and culture, not because age itself prevents or diminishes vitality. It is well documented that certain societies have vital, long-lived, and engaged aging populations. The Abklasia people of southern Russia and the long-lived elders in Okinawa, Japan are two examples. These societies nourish and relate to each other differently than we do. They also tend to expect to live well in loving community as they age. Respect and care for elders is a given.

So how do we begin to age with vitality? What does vital aging mean to the physical body? And what about the emotional, mental, and spiritual dimensions of vital aging? Physically, we notice one of the most common problems associated with age is painful joints and arthritis. By age forty, 90% of the population has some osteoarthritic changes visible on x-rays in the knees or hips. The effects of gravity on the body over time cause structural challenges. These challenges with structure and alignment can accelerate the degenerative process if they are not addressed. That feeling of dragging yourself out of bed, aching and stiff, is one of the hallmarks of feeling old. This is the result of inflammation in the body. Anti-inflammatory drugs only mask these symptoms and are not the answer. A whole systems approach is needed to stop or reverse inflammation. Arthritis can be healed with proper nourishment, alignment, and movement. The good news is that we know more today than ever before about how to support vital aging and reduce inflammation of all kinds.

Exciting new research has changed our understanding of what causes aging and how we might begin to maintain and/or increase physical vitality at every stage of life. Scientists have discovered that the length of protective "caps" at the end of our DNA, called telomeres (te-le-mir), predict how fast we will age. As we age, telomeres shorten. The protective cap is lost and the DNA starts to unravel. The longer your telomeres, the longer your lifespan, and the more chance you have to be disease free.

Remember the story of Ponce de Leon and his search for the fountain of youth? If that mythical fountain had been found you can bet that it was pouring forth a substance that lengthened telomeres. While we don't understand everything about telomeres at this point, there have been enough studies to make this one of the hottest research subjects in the field of longevity.

But even now, we do know something about what

sustains telomere length. And what we know is that all the choices we've discussed that support vitality also support telomere length. Movement, a pH balanced diet, regular meditation practice, and superfood supplements all support the length of your telomeres. Please see the Recommendations list at the end of this chapter if you would like to know more about specific supplements that specifically support telomere health. Regular chiropractic care can address the structural and alignment changes caused by gravity, trauma, and stress. These practices are the foundation for the vital aging experience.

And while our quality of life as we age is profoundly influenced by the state of our physical bodies, as Dr. Martinez points out, the state of our bodies is also influenced by our emotional, mental, social, cultural, and spiritual experiences and expectations. Our brains need to stay active as well as our bodies. Exposure to new ideas, conversations, and learning keeps our minds supple and healthy. We can choose to keep learning, moving, nourishing, and connecting as we age.

We can even decide not to participate in the popular cultural way of looking at aging. We can stop thinking that every ache or pain is a sign of getting old, or the harbinger of some catastrophic disease and instead view these signals as feedback. Asking "what is the body trying to tell me?" and responding with care creates a different experience than resigning oneself to inevitable decline. We can cultivate strong social networks and loving relationships with people of all ages. We can find purpose and joy in serving others and expressing our caring in the world. According to research cited by the Corporation for National and Community Services, volunteering and being of service extends the life and health of the volunteer. (Dulin and Hill, 2003; Brown et al., 2005; Brown et al., 2003; Liang et al., 2001; Morrow-Howell et al., 2003; Midlarsky and Kahana, 1994; and Schwartz et al., 2003) In fact, these studies show the benefits derived from serving. Those who give support through volunteering experience greater health benefits than those who receive support through these activities.

> For example: The results of a survey of a large, ethnically diverse sample of older adults showed no association between receiving social support and improved health; however, the study did find that those who gave social support to others had lower rates of mortality than those who did not, even when controlling for socioeconomic status,

education, marital status, age, gender, and ethnicity. (Brown et al., 2005)

Offering yourself in service is also an acknowledgement of the something bigger that connects us all. This brings us full circle back to our spiritual nature. Joy is available here without regard to age or ability. Yet the gift of age is such that regardless of belief or creed, facing our mortality as we age compels a new urgency to the most human of questions: Who am I and why am I here? Getting older can initiate a profound deepening into joyous vitality because aging occurs not just in the body, but also in the mind, heart and spirit. Connecting with Spiritual Intelligence as we age may look different for each individual, but vital aging is a holistic experience that is incomplete without a sense of the greater part of self.

A quick poll of women over forty reveals a variety of attitudes toward aging, from not being conscious of aging, feeling a spiritual process of getting younger rather than older, increased confidence and acceptance of changes in appearance, to the heightened awareness of impermanence. In each of these attitudes there is some opportunity to become even more fully present to life. If we choose to accept them, the gifts of vital aging must include a deepening into the awareness that we are more than a physical body. This is where Spiritual Intelligence and age collude to open you into your fullness. This is the place from where, if you choose to engage it, your unique history of being is available to be expressed as only YOU can, here and now.

Things to Remember:

Food from the Land-Fresh, organic, locally grown foods are more nutritionally dense, providing more nourishment. Avoid packaged, processed food-like substances, sugar and nutritionally deficient foods. Eat in alignment with the body's design.

Intermittent Fasting-If you have no health contraindications, try periodic fasting to let the body repair and cleanse, while reducing calories and burning fat.

Grass not Grain-If you eat animal protein sources, grass fed is both more humane for the animal, and the more alkalizing choice for your overall health.

Eat More Plants-Plants supply our bodies with the necessary phytonutrients for a healthy body but also keep our symbiotic microbiome healthy and growing. Plants should make up at least 70-75% of our nutritional intake. Local and organic is best.

Supplements-Do use high quality, food based nutritional supplements from the list in this chapter. Be sure to include high quality telomere support supplements,

Regular Movement-Our bodies are made to move. Move regularly in ways that you enjoy, which encourage you to move more often!

Maintain Nervous System Function-Your nervous system is the conductor of energy to and from Spiritual Intelligence. Regular chiropractic adjustments restore and maintain nervous system function.

Practice Positive Aging-Notice your beliefs about aging and whether they support the way you want to live as you age. Seek help and support for changing yo mindset when necessary, especially if you are being influenced by negative cultural messages about getting older. Embrace purposeful living through community service and nourishing relationships.

CHAPTER FIVE

Growing Loving Relationships

"We can live without religion and meditation, but we cannot survive without human affection."

-Dalai Lama

As we've mentioned before, Creative Self-Health is not just about caring for the physical body, but optimizing a state of being that includes the whole person, the greater self.. Individually, there is a lot we can do to support our own wellbeing. Yet we were designed so that our need for loving bonds with others is intrinsically tied to our overall health.

Without a sense of being worthy of love and respect, a sense of belonging in relationship to others, and a sense of purpose or connection with something bigger than our individual lives, human beings fail to experience optimal health.

The fact is, developing healthy relationships of all kinds-with self, friends, family, community, and a trusted team of health care advisors- is critical to health and well-being. The depth of commitment we bring to this process is also a reflection of our growing alignment with Spiritual Intelligence.

Befriending Yourself

Taking charge of your relationship with yourself is one of the foundations of health. It may seem like an odd idea, but developing and maintaining a friendly relationship with yourself can be more challenging than it seems on the surface. This is especially true if you are struggling with a history of abuse or other life trauma.

For some, just noticing how you speak to yourself inside your own head can be revealing. Are you someone who has a very active inner critic? The voice of negativity and judgment about yourself often acts as if it's only giving you helpful advice or feedback, when in truth you would never speak to anyone else in your life the way you speak to yourself. Do you hold yourself to standards of perfection that are unrealistic? Do you expect yourself to never make a mistake? Do you criticize yourself mercilessly when you fall short of your own standards?

These are far too common symptoms of an unsupportive relationship to self that often manifests physically as chronic stress. Here's a little secret about that inner critic: you don't have to believe what it says. You can choose instead to treat yourself at least as well as you would treat any other friend you value.

Making a choice to start treating yourself with kindness can happen even if you are having trouble believing you are worth it. Developing a more loving relationship with self can be a lifelong project, but growing in compassion, forgiveness, and friendliness toward self is worth the commitment. Scientists such as Professor Richie Davidson, the William James and Vilas Professor of Psychology and Psychiatry at the University of Wisconsin-Madison, have studied the connection between emotions and brain activity. Professor Davidson's extensive work in the area known as affective neuroscience (how emotions effect brain structure and function) confirms that emotional states such as kindness and compassion can structurally change the brain. Professor Davidson has also documented how meditation can positively transform the brain.

With patience and persistence, befriending yourself will reshape your brain's neural pathways, allowing the inner critic to give way to the inner healer. Your alignment with Spiritual Intelligence grows, and your capacity for rich and loving relationships of all kinds increases.

The Need to Belong

We are designed to thrive in community. A sense of belonging is a basic human need. Human beings are herd animals who require the warm comfort of touch, the recognition of being seen and heard as important by another, and the sense of belonging to a loving community.

It seems that warm social relationships are essential to health and longevity, and science supports this fact. The "Roseto Effect" refers to the results of a study conducted by researchers on a small community of Italian-Americans in Roseto, Pennsylvania, who defied every standard of modern healthy living relating to diet, exercise, smoking, etc., yet were consistently long lived. The intensive study revealed one factor as the cause for this. As noted by Dr. Rock Positano:

> "Rosetans, regardless of income and education, expressed themselves in a family-

centered social life. There was a total absence of ostentation among the wealthy, meaning that those who had more money didn't flaunt it. Families were close knit, self-supportive and independent, but also relied-in bad times-on the greater community for well-defined assistance and friendly help. No one was alone in Roseto. No one seemed too unhappy or too stressed out. And the proof was a heart attack /death rate almost half of everyone else around them. Each house contained three families, or three generations. The elderly were neither institutionalized nor marginalized, but were "installed" as informal judges and arbitrators in everyday life and commerce."

The importance of healthy relationship to physical health and longevity is also cited by a study through Brigham Young University that concludes that the protective effects of having lots of healthy, fulfilling relationships are comparable to that of quitting smoking. Additionally, strong social ties consistently predict longer life spans.

One example from our own practice is" Steven". Steven had spent most of his adult life married to the same woman. Like many aged widowers, when his wife died, he become more socially isolated with each year that passed. He had outlived most of his family and friends.

Year after year, Steven remained alone. Now in his mid nineties, he was less healthy, more fragile with age and the expected physical and mental decline. Eventually, Steven suffered a stroke that sent him to the hospital. It seemed clear that the end was near and the medical staff that cared for him tried to make him as comfortable as possible.

But to everyone's surprise, Steven began to recover physically from his stroke. He was still fragile, and in order for Steven to continue in his home, he was given twenty-four-hour nursing care.

Now, for the first time in years, Steven is never alone. There is always someone there to listen to him, prepare his meals, and offer companionship. When his doctors see him now, they notice that while he still has difficulty moving around, his mind is clear, and he is alert and engaged with life. Before his stroke, Steven had been afraid and resistant to having strangers caring for him, but now he is happier and considers his nursing care team his best friends.

Many of us know someone like Steven, who was brought back from the brink with human contact and care. We intuitively understand the power of belonging, feeling valued, and loved. This is why community means more than just the people who live in your neighborhood. Choosing community is part of Creative Self-Health. You choose to activate community with those people who see and honor you for who you are. We know that social isolation leads to ill health and depression. The evidence all points to loving connection with a partner, friends, and community as a far more effective remedy for depression and isolation than medication.

The paradox of healthy living is that even as we commit to self-healing, we cannot do it alone. We need each other in order to be whole.

Developing Healthy Relationships

What is a healthy relationship? Healthy relationships feel good most of the time. There is a sense of increased life energy and enjoyment in the exchange between friends. Understanding and respect are present even when there is disagreement. Mistakes and conflict are acknowledged and worked through. In short, healthy relationships, whether with friends or romantic partners, are enriching rather than draining.

So how do we get to health in our relationships? As we've mentioned, we start with committing to a healthy relationship with Self. This involves all the self-care practices outlined in this book, including getting professional help where needed.

As self-care deepens, the natural desire to connect with others in a healthy way is strengthened. Many of us will already have at least one or two supportive, caring relationships in our lives. Being grateful for those relationships is a practice we recommend.

On the other hand, it is not uncommon for there to be some long-standing relationships in our lives that are not as healthy or supportive as we would like them to be. Sometimes sharing your concerns with another can inspire change and the relationship will grow as a result.

Then there are the moments when Spiritual Intelligence will nudge you to accept that someone in your life who was a friend is not able or willing to support your new level of healthy living. You may choose to keep this friend in your life in a limited way, or you may need to let go of the relationship if you find it to be more draining than enriching. It is your commitment to your own healing that will guide you through this painful but necessary experience.

It is necessary to be discerning about the people we

let into our lives and the people we want to keep close to us. Those who align with the values of health and healing enrich us. Letting go of draining relationships is a Self-Health practice. Even as you grieve the loss of what was, you are practicing a healthier way of relating, first to yourself, then to all others.

This is true whether the relationship is with a friend, a romantic partner, or even a family member. Just as with relating differently to yourself, developing healthy relationships takes time, commitment, and support. This is why your Self-Health journey is incomplete without a team of advisors to assist you.

Your Team of Advisors

Taking charge of your health requires a different attitude toward the healthcare professionals in your life. Creative Self-Health is a multi-dimensional, dynamic and evolving journey. It encompasses your mind, body, and spirit. Your team of advisors are the professionals you hire to assist you with each and all of those aspects of your health. They are there to support your vitality as a whole person.

From this perspective, an annual check-up or traditional preventative care just won't suffice. Who will you choose for your team of healthcare advisors?

And why?

Your choices may change depending on what stage of life and health you are in currently. Thinking proactively about your need for a certain type of advisor is a Self-Health practice. For instance, if you are a forty-seven year old woman who is athletic, works in a high stress field, and is experiencing peri-menopausal symptoms you would need a different support team than a thirty year old smoker who wants to prepare for a healthy pregnancy.

And of course, you are probably not starting from scratch. You may already have a medical doctor, a dentist, and some other support such as a personal trainer. The shift here is in how you think about these people and the roles they play in your life. Have you considered the gaps in the team you have currently?

Some possible additions to your team could include a chiropractor, acupuncturist, yoga teacher, spiritual advisor or financial coach. Therapists, homeopathic doctors, nutritionists, herbalists, etc. can all be candidates for your team at certain times and stages of life.

And the key advisors on your team don't have to cost anything. Just about everyone can benefit from a team that includes a wise mentor and a place for accountability. For some, that mentor could be a respected parent or grandparent who will listen and give advice when asked. Others may meet regularly with a group of supportive friends. The mentoring relationship can be reciprocal or not. What's important is that your mentor has the knowledge, wisdom, and willingness to support you and to help you stay accountable to what you want to accomplish.

That said, it is you who must take action to engage this type of support person or persons on a regular basis.

Your team is just that-*your* team. These are the professionals you hire to give you expert advice and guidance as you embrace healthy living. You have the right to choose those who best serve you and the responsibility to make staffing changes when necessary. What do you need from your team? Who will you choose to help you live with vitality?

Things to Remember:

Practice Being a Friend to Yourself-Continue daily meditation. Meditation trains you to observe your thoughts, including self-critical thoughts. Being aware is the first step toward healing. When the inner critic is attacking, challenge it! Actively tell yourself you don't have to believe what it says. Then focus compassion on the part of you that feels attacked and hurt. According to research by Professor Tor Wager at the University of Colorado in Boulder, compassionate awareness changes the way your brain works, steering it toward reduced stress and relaxation. Add a professional who is skilled in this area to your team of advisors if needed.

Incorporate the Creative Self-Health Daily Practice into your life-Review this practice in the section following the Appendix at end of the book.

Let Go of Draining Relationships When Necessary- It may not be easy, so gather your community, a professional on your team of advisors, and your mentor to help give you extra support if needed. Be gentle with yourself and give yourself permission to grieve the loss of a relationship and your hopes for that relationship. Write a letter to yourself about why you are choosing to let go and give yourself encouragement. With time, the opening that was a loss will become an opportunity for a more enriching relationship to enter your life.

Learn About Healthy Partnership-Do you know anyone who is happily married or partnered? Ask them about how it works for them. Be curious and open about what is shared. If there is a relationship in your life that works very well, think about why it works for you. What are your values when it comes to relationship? How can you bring more of what you value to your current relationships with friends, family, or partner?

Look for Supportive Community Connections- Spend some time thinking about your needs in terms of a supportive community. Whether it's something as structured as a 12 Step program or just a shared meal with some friends, build regular community time into your life. And while an online community can be helpful, the optimal Self-Health community recommendation is for an in person support system.

Add This Professional to Your Team of Advisors-As described in earlier chapters, the nervous system is the connector between the physical and non-physical. Keeping the nervous system functioning without interference allows clear communication with Spiritual Intelligence in both directions. Remember to support your connection to Spiritual Intelligence by adding a Chiropractor to your team of advisors.

Be Receptive to Spiritual Intelligence-Supporting your physical body, being friendly toward yourself and forgiving of your mistakes are all wonderful activities for feeding your connection with Spiritual Intelligence. But it is your willingness to know yourself as Spiritual Intelligence that makes the difference between simply feeling good and experiencing wholeness.

When you open your heart and mind to Spiritual Intelligence, you begin to experience yourself as part of something bigger than your individual life. You know you are more than a physical body, not because this book says so, but because you have experienced the truth of that knowing. Your capacity to live fully as who you really are is ignited. In our final chapter, we will explore what it means to move beyond Self-Health into Self-Mastery, and why this movement can change the world.

CHAPTER SIX

Emerging into Self-Mastery

*"The first peace, which is the most important, is that
which comes within the souls of people when they
realize their relationship, their oneness with the
universe and all its powers, and when they realize
that at the center of the universe dwells the Great
Spirit, and that this center is really everywhere, it is
within each of us."*

-Black Elk

What is the impact of practicing Creative Self-Health as a regular way of life? Lori gives us a real life glimpse into the possibilities:

I love soccer, and have played for many years. A few years back, my team was playing against another team that had an overly aggressive style. One of their team members kicked me, causing my ankle to twist with a really bad sprain. By that evening, the ankle was swollen and the pain was awful. I took some of the natural remedies I knew would help, but ankle sprains take awhile to heal.

I was scheduled to leave the next day for a conference for health practitioners like myself who use a bio energetic technique to clear emotional and mental blocks to healing. The plane left in the morning, but I could barely walk on the ankle. I limped into the airport determined to make the best of things, but realized that my layover at the Los Angeles terminal would require me to walk a long distance in order to transfer to the next plane. There was no way I could make it to the scheduled gate.

I had to ask for a wheelchair and assistance to get there in time for my flight. After I landed, my roommate for the conference, another practitioner, immediately gave me a treatment. The emotional block that she uncovered was judgment. Well, I was definitely having a hard time with anger and judging that other soccer player for injuring me! I was upset because there is no reason for that type of playing. My roommate's treatment was supposed to help me clear the judgment, but it was 11:00 pm and we had to get up early the next day for the conference, so I just went to bed.

The next morning my ankle was still hurting and swollen but I made my way down to the conference. Supported by being in the healing community of practitioners, I began to focus my attention on clearing the emotional block that we'd uncovered the night before.

I spent the morning letting go of anger, bringing in forgiveness, and finally placing a deep attention on gratitude for a fully functioning, healed and pain-free ankle. The depth of feeling I experienced is hard to describe. There was crystal clarity of my intention and in awhile I began to feel the physical clearing in my body, not in my ankle but in my heart and gut. It was amazing!

My roommate did one more brief treatment for me that afternoon, and when I got up from the table we both saw that my ankle was no longer swollen. There was no pain. I was able to attend the rest of the conference as if the ankle sprain had never happened. It was completely healed. I myself have treated many sprained ankles over the years and they took at least a week or two to heal, but this happened in a matter of hours. On the return flight, I found myself in Los Angeles again, but this time I walked through the long stretch between terminals without any problem.

Experiences like the one Lori describes are instances of Self-Mastery. These are the quantum moments when your Self-Health practice leads you into complete alignment with Spiritual Intelligence, resulting in healing at a level beyond the ordinary. Lori's story couldn't have happened without the work she had put into Self-Health practices before her ankle was sprained. She already believed in the power of the body to heal itself. She was able to access a deep place of emotional healing because she had long been committed to meditation, forgiveness, gratitude, and other types of Self-Health practices as a part of her daily life.

Living as Spiritual Intelligence

At the beginning of this book, we discussed some of the science behind quantum physics. As you will recall, quantum physics supports our belief that each human being is a projection emanating from Spiritual Intelligence. This works in much the same way biology tells us that we start out as one cell that then divides over and over again to eventually form the fingers, toes, eyes, and other parts of one human being. These different parts are all created with the same unique blueprint (DNA) yet do not look alike. Your fingers do not look like your eyes, yet they are made with the same basic materials. Some inherent intelligence in the DNA cues the cells to differentiate into the needed parts. This biological process mimics the way that Spiritual Intelligence creates individual human bodies using itself as the blueprint. Spiritual Intelligence is immense and infinite in nature. It is the highest vibration of energy. As it projects part of itself outward, it begins to slow its vibratory rate until finally it appears like solid mass. The human body is such a mass, projected from and composed of Spiritual Intelligence, slowed down into physical form. Every molecule that makes up the physical body contains within it the emotional, mental and energetic vibrations of Spiritual Intelligence. You can picture this much like ice, water, and steam are all the same molecule but vibrating at different rates.

This is how you are more than a physical body. Since the nature of Spiritual Intelligence is infinite, there are an infinite number of ways that this Intelligence can express itself as individual human experience. Each of us is unique, part of Spiritual Intelligence condensed into material form. Your unique design includes the energies of the personality, and is influenced by the set of circumstances, conditions, time, place and culture into which you were born.

At the start of the Creative Self-Health journey, there is often a period of simply learning from a cognitive point of view about health, healing, greater Self, etc. This learning is good and necessary, but not the same as starting to practice the tools of Self-Health.

As the tools are practiced, experiences of self-care and self-healing begin to affect changes in the quality of daily life. New, empowering beliefs start to become more real. You begin to know how to manage your emotional states, how to choose healing even under difficult circumstances. These shifts are most often experienced as a type of moving through cycles. It is normal to have moments or weeks of feeling empowered followed by a seeming fall back into old patterns and behavior. You will cycle through many layers of growth and sometimes feel as if you have made no real progress. Moments of mastery are followed by moments of being all too human. Yet, gradually you will notice yourself responding differently to situations and/or people than you have in the past. You will see yourself relating to the greater part of you in a different way. You are embracing the full spectrum of your life, with all its emotional ups and downs, in gratitude.

Changing the World from the Inside Out

Each of us alive today reading these words has been born during a pivotal moment in human history. Although our individual human journeys are unique, at the same time, as the ancients have always said, we are all one. We are all composed of the same basic high levels of energetic vibration that is Spiritual Intelligence. This includes all aspects of the natural world we inhabit. Animals, plants, the planet itself are all composed from the same basic energetic material.

Our connection to each other and all that is through Spiritual Intelligence means that in addition to being more than a physical body, we are also more than an individual life. We are a part of a creative emergence and expansion that cannot be defined by an individual life. Paradoxically, there is something about experiencing this greater connectivity that catalyzes individual life purpose.

The mission that is authentically yours, whether it is expressed through a career, a vocation, or simply being a good neighbor, is revealed as you become more open to yourself as Spiritual Intelligence. The world we live in needs each of us living from our sense of purpose if we are to navigate the immense challenges before us. The greater part of us profoundly understands our personal health is bound to the health and wellbeing of the whole planet.

This is why purpose is often expressed through service in various forms. In a way, all Self-Health practices are acts of service to the expanding expression of Spiritual Intelligence within. It is natural for this service orientation to develop as you move closer to Self-Mastery, relating to the external world as an expression of Spiritual Intelligence. On the physical level, service is also linked with longevity. According to a 2007 article from the Corporation for National and Community Service:

> "The results of a survey of a large, ethnically diverse sample of older adults showed no association between receiving social support and improved health; however, the study did find that those who gave social support to others had lower rates of mortality than those who did not, even when controlling for socioeconomic status, education, marital status, age, gender, and ethnicity. (Brown et al., 2005)"

Service, purpose and meaning are integrated as you continue to connect with your greater self. Self-

Health practices that enhance awareness and openness bring you to a point where it is possible to have a quantum moment like the one Lori describes. In this quantum moment, it all comes together in a miraculous way and you KNOW yourself as much more than a physical body. Your knowing tells you that anything is possible. This is Self-Mastery, when Spiritual Intelligence is a lived experience, not just a nice theory. Praying for others, or reaching out to others happens through the lens of your Greater Self. Toni shares an experience of intentional connecting through this lens:

> I had purchased an item earlier in the day from a store clerk whose attitude had been abrupt and harsh. All my attempts at pleasantries were met with irritation and I was relieved to leave. A friend who was with me said later that the clerk had a reputation for being unpleasant, so I was doubly happy to have concluded my business with her and made a mental note never to return to the store.
>
> Unfortunately, when I looked at the receipt I saw that the clerk had made an error and charged me for an additional different item that I did not purchase. By this time it was evening and the store was closed, but I needed to correct the error. I had no real

proof that the error had been made, as the clerk could easily decide I was lying and had not been charged incorrectly. I dreaded seeing the clerk again, and as I sat in meditation with my own discomfort I realized this was an opportunity to connect with the clerk's Greater Self to ask for help with the situation.

I began to focus my attention on the clerk as Spiritual Intelligence and to communicate with that part of her. I explained my dilemma to her Greater Self and asked for help and an easy resolution.

I concentrated on feeling connected to the clerk, letting my anxieties about seeing her again dissolve and replacing them with feelings of confidence and ease.

The next morning I woke still feeling positive and calm. When I approached the clerk, she listened to me explain what had happened and immediately corrected the mistake. Something had shifted enough so that the interaction between us was completely different than the day before, and I left feeling gratitude for the experience.

The shift that Toni is describing is possible when we change our thoughts and feelings (in this case from dread to confidence and ease) and then engage on a deeper level with the perception of Intelligence that permeates everyone and everything. For some, this happens through prayer, or compassionate awareness, or just offering good wishes to another.

The acknowledgement of the Greater Self in others is the basis for social justice and other acts of love that change the world from the inside out.

Reaching Mastery

No one can explain or predict when a quantum moment will occur. What we can do is help prepare you for that time, like a gardener preparing the soil in a way that best nurtures the seeds that will soon be planted.

Self Mastery is a state wherein our physical, energetic, and spiritual selves are aligned. In this state, we are receptive to the intelligence that spirit continually offers us. Through our personal growth, we become available to consciously offer our experiences and perceptions in the material world back to Spiritual Intelligence. This state is sometimes called being in the flow, or in the zone. As golfer Sam Snead expresses it, "Being in the zone is about moving from powerful effort to finding your effortless power."

Physically, this means the brain and nervous system are functioning optimally in their role as the interface between our perceptions (expressed as thoughts, beliefs, and emotions) and experiences in the material world and the greater reality of Spiritual Intelligence. Spiritual guidance in the form of intuition, gut feelings, dreams, and heartfelt desires are felt through the nervous system. Our perceptions and experiences are relayed to Spiritual Intelligence via the nervous system and brain. Artists and other creative types feel the flow or zone as inspiration for their work. It is the source of much great art, feats of Olympic athleticism, and sociopolitical progress. We are all capable of accessing this source.

And we will all continue to experience being knocked off balance at times. Self-Mastery is about gaining the capacity, strength, and skill to navigate back to the zone after a setback. But how do we get there? All the practices explained in this book will not help unless they are consistently practiced. You and you alone must choose to commit to taking charge of your life and your health. You must decide to be responsible and accountable for what you choose. Like any challenging journey, there will be moments along the way when persistence and courage are needed to take the next step. It is crucial to have a support team, people you trust, people who care about you, and people who have the expertise to serve you when needed.

As you continue the journey, you will more and more often experience the wisdom, inspiration, and guidance of Spiritual Intelligence. You will feel humility, joy, and awe as your Greater Self is revealed. Your connection to Spiritual Intelligence becomes an embodiment of unconditional love. The depth of being you bring to any situation is fed by this connection. This is living as Spiritual Intelligence. It can be scary to start something new, but our hope is that this book will help encourage you to begin. It is our greatest wish for you that you choose to live fully, in health, joy, and unconditional love. May you live as the One Spiritual Intelligence that the world so needs

I AM ONE

I am One.

I am one with my lover, I am one with my son, I am one with my daughter.

I am One

I am one with my sister, I am one with my brother, I am one with my neighbor.

I am One.

I am one with all creatures, I am one with all flowers, I am one with all trees.

I am One.

I am one with the mountains, I am one with the rivers, I am one with the oceans.

I am One.

I am one with the earth, I am one with the sun, I am one with the stars.

I am One.

I am one with the galaxy, I am one with the universe, I am one with the light.

I am One.

I am one with all healing, I am one with all pe-ace, I am one with all lo-ove.

I am One.

I am one with Go-od, I am one with Go-od, I am one with Go-od

I am one with Spirit, I am one with Spirit, I am one with Spirit.

I am One.

-Lori-Ann Gertonson

APPENDIX

If you are interested in exploring the concepts and suggestions presented in this book and would like more personal assistance with implementing them in your life, you may want to consider working with Dr. Gertonson directly. She has developed The Quantum Alignment Process™ (QAP), a powerful, effective system for restoring health, promoting wellbeing and creating wholeness in your life. It is process of releasing the barriers to health, recreating a new more vital state of being and reconnecting to a larger sense of what is possible for your life. It is Creative Self-Health in action. It is a consciousness based healing system rooted in neuroscience, quantum physics, and spirituality.

The program is based on four foundations of Creative Self-Health.

1. Meditation and Visualization - to cultivate balance and to connect to Spiritual Intelligence.
2. Stress Management- to learn how to regulate your system for positive outcomes.
3. Essentials of Letting Go-a process for releasing limiting beliefs and other barriers to peace and happiness.
4. Healthy Lifestyle and Vitality-guidance to transition from unsupportive lifestyle habits to new supportive habits.

Dr. Gertonson has helped many people to navigate life transitions with ease, to restore hope and a sense of "self" again, and to create their optimal life experience using the Quantum Alignment Process™. There are 3 parts to the process:

1. Private sessions with a Creative Self-Health Professional
2. Creative Self-Health home program
3. Foundations of Creative Self-Health group sessions

Dr. Gertonson is available for consultation and can be reached through her website at

www.tgiwellness.com

Research has shown that if you follow a daily practice for at least sixty-six days, it will become a regular habit and you will see your life change. Consistency is the key here. Deciding once to embark on this practice with joy in your heart and applying it daily with discipline whether your mood feels like it or not is what will signal the change. It is one of the greatest gifts you can give yourself. If you want to get a quick start to Creative Self-Health on your own, then we suggest following the Creative Self-Health Daily Practice on the following pages.

CREATIVE SELF-HEALTH

CREATIVE SELF-HEALTH DAILY PRACTICE

MEDITATE every day (preferably in the morning after awakening) for 15-20 minutes to allow yourself to quiet your mind and calm the body. As you do this you connect and align with your Spiritual Intelligence and set yourself up for an inspired day seeing and feeling what is truly possible for you.

APPRECIATION AND GRATITUDE-Spend a few moments every morning focused on gratitude for someone or something in your life. Sit with the feeling until you truly "feel" the gratitude in your heart. Placing your hand over your heart while you do this exercise will greatly enhance the experience.

Writing in a journal especially in the evening before bed a list of all the positive things you feel appreciative of in your life. Without judgment or too much thinking, just write a list, however long. Then spend a moment to read over and feel the appreciation in your heart.

SELF LOVE-Affirm self-love and self-acceptance.. Appreciate and affirm yourself and your greatness. (For example, I am loveable, I am worthy, I love and accept myself just as I am, etc.)

As you say these affirmations out loud, hold yourself in a personal embrace. Cross your arms over your heart giving yourself a hug! (And if you cross your legs too you will communicate with both sides of your brain and Spiritual Intelligence more easily.)

CONNECT TO THE GREATER PART OF YOURSELF-Acknowledge Spiritual Intelligence and its assistance and guidance in your life. Feel the inner knowing and connection to this greater part of yourself.

CONNECT TO NATURE-Find time each day to connect to nature, and the oneness of all that is. Find time to really "see" the natural world around you and acknowledge the beauty of the world. You can watch the birds, the trees in the wind, the flowers in the garden, the clouds in the sky, or ocean waves, etc. Read the 'I am One' poem in chapter six.

ENDNOTES

Brown, William Michael et al, Altruism Relates to Health in an Ethnically Diverse Sample of Older Adults, The Journals of Gerontology: Series B, Volume 60, Issue 3, May 2005, Pages P143–P152,

Cook Schoffro, Michelle, *The Ultimate pH Solution*, New York, HarperCollins, 2008

Corporation for National and Community Service, Office of Research and Policy Development. Volunteering in America: 2007 City Trends and Rankings, Washington, DC 2007.

Dulin, P., & Hill, R. (2003). Relationships between Altruistic Activity and Positive and Negative Affect among Low-Income Older Adult Service Providers. Aging & Mental Health, 7(4): 294–299.

Hay, Louise, *You Can Heal Your Life.* Hay House, 1999

Liang, J., Krause, N. M., & Bennett, J. M. (2001). "Social Exchange and Well-Being: Is Giving Better than Receiving?" Psychology and Aging, 16(3): 511–523

Midlarsky, E., & Kahana, E. (1994). Sage library of social research, Vol. 196. Altruism in later life. Thousand Oaks, CA, US: Sage Publications, Inc.

Morrow-Howell et al (2003) Effects of Volunteering on the Well-Being of Older Adult

The Journals of Gerontology: Series *B*, Volume 58, Issue 3, May 2003, Pages S137–S145,

Positano, Dr. Rock, The Mystery of the Rosetan People. Huffington Post 03/28/2008: Updated November 17, 2011

Schwartz, C., Meisenhelder, J. B., Ma, Y., & Reed, G. (2003). Altruistic social interest behaviors are associated with better mental health. Psychosomatic Medicine, 65, 778–785.

https://news.byu.edu/news/prescription-living-longer-spend-less-time-alone

ABOUT THE AUTHORS

Dr. Lori-Ann Gertonson

Dr. Lori-Ann Gertonson is a practicing wholistic chiropractor and the founder of The Gertonson Institute, an integrative wellness center. She developed the Quantum Alignment Process,™ a consciousness-based healing system rooted in neuroscience, quantum physics, and spirituality. In addition to being a doctor of chiropractic, she holds certifications in various areas of health and healing.

For over 35 years, she has helped individuals to heal and release physical pain, anxiety, and overwhelm in their lives, to create happiness in daily life, and to navigate life transitions with ease while connecting to a deeper sense of self and higher purpose.

She has incorporated all this experience into the theory and practice of Creative Self-Health. She is passionate about bringing a new perspective to healthcare by providing the knowledge and tools for people to take charge of their own health and healing, live well, and connect to Spiritual Intelligence. It is her goal to help people create a healthy, happy life feeling "alive" all the years of their life.

Toni Mandara

After leaving a career in hospital work, Toni Mandara began to study diverse yet interconnected integrative healing pathways through dreamwork, trauma recovery, somatic movement, West African storytelling, personality typing, shamanic practices, and Buddhist inquiry. She became a meditation group facilitator and a life coach incorporating all these teachings into a synthesis she calls Somatic Process Healing. Today she is a writer and Somatic Process facilitator. Her decades of training and experience in both the conventional medical world and integrative health form a rich backdrop for her perspective on health and healing.

She has a private practice at The Gertonson Institute in Albany, California, that supports young adults involved in social justice and climate change movements to integrate individual and collective healing into their work. When not at the office, she can be found at work on her second book exploring the experiences of Black women practicing culturally supportive forms of Creative Self-Health.

Thank you for reading our book. If you enjoyed it, won't you please take a moment to leave us a review at your favorite retailer?

Thanks!

-Lori-Ann and Toni

Made in the USA
Las Vegas, NV
12 September 2022

55190661R00083